CW00432763

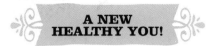

A NEW
HEALTHY YOU!

5:2 Diet

igloobooks

igloobooks

Published in 2017
by Igloo Books Ltd
Cottage Farm
Sywell
NN6 0BJ
www.igloobooks.com

Copyright © 2017 Igloo Books Ltd

All rights reserved. No part of this publication may be
reproduced or transmitted in any form or by any means,
electronic, or mechanical, including photocopying, recording,
or by any information storage and retrieval system,
without permission in writing from the publisher.
The measurements used are approximate.

Cover images: (tr) Line Klein / © Getty images,(bl) Sian Irvine / © Getty images
Additional cover and interior imagery: © iStock / Getty images

HUN001 1017
2 4 6 8 10 9 7 5 3 1
ISBN 978-1-78810-616-0

Cover designed by Nicholas Gage
Edited by Jasmin Peppiatt

Printed and manufactured in China

Contents

Introduction

When you want to lose a few pounds, you want to do it as effortlessly as possible, right? You don't want to have to buy special foods or branded goods that involve counting units or restrict you from eating the things that you love every single day of the week. And most of all, you don't want it to take up all of your time.

This plan is different. It is also incredibly simple.

For five days of the week, you can eat whatever you like within the recommended guidelines of up to 2000 calories per day for women or up to 2500 calories per day for men. So, you can have your usual breakfast, lunch and dinner with snacks in between. On two other days per week, you restrict yourself to 500 calories per day for women or 600 calories per day for men.

This 5:2 combination (five days off dieting and two days on) can help you with gradual weight loss that is easy to manage for as long as you want to lose weight.

Intermittent fasting has been around for centuries – now is the time to make it work for you!

The science of fasting

The idea of using fasting days to lose weight first reached the general public via a BBC Horizon documentary called 'Eat, Fast and Live Longer', shown on television in 2012.

It is based on the principle called Intermittent Fasting (IF). Put simply, you eat normally on certain days and fast on others. It has its roots in the days of early man, when hunter-gatherers would go for lengthy periods without eating while searching for food.

The theory is that being hungry made man's brain sharper and, therefore, he was better able to hunt the food needed to stave off hunger pangs. Back in the days of cave-dwellers, it would have been quite normal for people to go hungry for several hours, before feasting on whatever they managed to catch. Early man would have naturally practised intermittent fasting but would probably never have gone more than a day before refuelling.

Fans of this way of eating claim that, as well as helping people lose weight, the 5:2 diet can offer other health benefits including increased life-span, protection from certain diseases and improved cognitive function. Currently, there is a limited body of evidence about intermittent fasting. But, as this way of eating becomes more popular, there is likely to be more scientific research into the area.

There have been some studies into the effectiveness of the 5:2 diet. In one study, researchers discovered that women on a 5:2 diet achieved similar levels of weight loss as women on a calorie-controlled diet.

They also found reductions in some biological indicators or biomarkers that suggest a reduction in the risk of developing chronic conditions such as type 2 diabetes.

The ancient art of fasting

Fasting is not a modern invention

For thousands of years, fasting – or abstaining from food or certain types of food – has been used as a way to cleanse the body, open the mind and give the faster an increased sense of wellbeing. It has been observed on all continents and in many religions and cultures.

Even before that, early man would have fasted as part of every day life. Like most animals, he would have had fasting enforced on him at some point – during times of stress, illness or food shortage. We all know people who go off their food at the smallest sign of uneasiness. That tendency to stop eating for a while is the body's way of seeking to rest, balance and conserve energy until it is needed most.

Fasting has its formal origins in serving the metaphysical needs of people. In its earliest usage, it was thought to be good for purifying the soul, for penance, mental clarity and redemption. This was when it was used for religious or cultural reasons rather than as a weight loss programme.

The roots: religious

Fasting has long been used in many religions, from Hinduism, Islam and Buddhism to Christianity, Mormonism and Judaism.

It is seen as an important part of religious practice, with many fasting days and periods throughout the calendar. Depending on the religion followed, certain foods, drinks and other substances are limited or avoided.

In Islam, Muslims fast for one month each year during Ramadan. This action serves as a reminder of the time when the Qur'an was revealed to Muhammad after he fasted. The aim is to prove devotion to Allah as well as discipline and conscientiousness of faith. In Islam, fasting is one of the so-called five pillars of Islam.

Fasting also has its place in both Jewish and Christian religions. Moses fasted for 40 days on Mount Sinai. Jesus fasted and prayed for 40 days in the wilderness. Today, Christians mark the Passion of Christ with Lent, a 40-day period before Easter when parishioners are encouraged to give something up for Lent and donate as much money as they can to charity.

The Jewish calendar has six days of fasting. The most well-known and most important is Yom Kippur, the day of reconciliation.

DO WE NEED SUGAR?

Calories are a measure of the energy a food contains. Sugar provides energy that we need, but it is only one source of energy. We should aim to get most of our calories from other foods, such as lean proteins, starchy foods and fruits and vegetables.

In ancient Greece, there was ritual fasting. This took place during the Eleusinian Mysteries to honour Demeter, the goddess of fertility. And other notable names, including Cicero, were known to have fasted in a bid to increase their mental performance.

As recently as the 20th century, Mahatma Gandhi, the father of the Indian independence movement, popularised fasting across India and around the world as a means of promoting passive resistance.

He went on a fast on behalf of the 'untouchables' in India. And he also publicly fasted for Hindus and Muslims to work peacefully side by side. This very peaceful form of protest has been used by many people across the globe to make their point to the powers that be.

The roots: medical

Although fasting began for religious and cultural reasons, people rapidly recognised that it had some medical benefits.

Hippocrates believed that fasting had 'miraculous' healing powers. He used certain foods to treat specific ailments. Greek philosopher Plato was known to have fasted for mental and physical efficiency. They believed that fasting could heal the body and spirit.

Mathematician and philosopher Pythagoras asked his followers to stick to a 40-day fast as he felt it improved mental perception and creativity. Then, 600 years later, Roman doctor Galen, believed that fasting was an effective therapy for keeping bodily fluids in equilibrium. Later on, during the 16th century, Paracelsus believed the body's functions could be correctly relegated by the use of fasting.

The roots: cultural

Many cultures have historically incorporated fasting into their way of life. Native American Indians would often fast prior to their sacred ceremonies. It was often used as an offering to the Great Spirit.

Fasting would be used at various times throughout the year and at important moments, such as the onset of puberty or prior to marriage. Native Americans believed that a fast cleansed the mind and body, freeing them to understand omens of good fortune from the Great Spirit.

Some devotees of yoga also use fasting methods that date back thousands of years. Yogi, Paramahansa Yogananda, believed that fasting was a natural method of healing and even today the practice of Ayurveda includes fasting as a form of therapy.

Why fasting works

Eating the 5:2 way can work for weight loss on many levels. If you go on a 'standard' weight loss diet, you need to cut down around 3,500 calories in order to lose a pound in weight. Reducing your daily calorie intake by 500 calories could mean that you would therefore lose one pound per week.

Eating plans like this, where you are dieting all the time, can lead to feelings of deprivation and a tendency to slip. Anyone who has tried to diet 24/7 knows that it can be a long slog – especially with our hectic lifestyles where food seems to tempt us every step of the way.

With the 5:2 approach, you just need to get yourself into the mindset that you only have to cut right down for two days out of every seven. In reality, it's just one day of restricted eating before you can eat normally again.

Many people find it comparatively easy to get through the fast days – they even find that they have no desire to splurge and scoff themselves on the other five days of the week.

And only 'being good' for two days out of a week is a much more manageable concept than feeling you have to watch what you're eating every single day in order to lose weight.

It can take you a few weeks to get into the 5:2 groove, but lots of people find that it works well for them.

It's easy to plan around your lifestyle too. Whereas 'full-time' dieting requires times when you are compromised by the food situations around you – birthday buffets, nights out, festive parties – the 5:2 approach means you can pick your fast days around your schedule.

Easy to plan

You can choose your fast days to fit around you. That's the wonderful thing about the 5:2 diet – you tailor-make it to your way of life, your work and home commitments. It's just about the most personalised diet there can be. As you'll see from the recipes in this book, there is so much flexibility in what you choose to eat. All the recipes state the calorie count too, so it's easy for you to track and add up the calories you've consumed.

The only real rules to this diet are that you restrict yourself to 500 calories for women or 600 calories for men over two non-consecutive days of the week. Whether that be a Monday and Thursday or a Tuesday and Saturday, it's entirely up to you!

If you're worried that you'll be fine all day long and then get the bedtime munchies, restrict your food during the day and eat something later so that you don't go to bed feeling deprived.

The 5:2 diet is great because – unless you want to shout it from the rooftops – people don't need to know that you're on a diet at all. And that can be good for many reasons. You don't have to listen to the diet saboteurs who tell you it'll never work or that you don't need to lose weight. You can choose your fast days to be times when you'd have time to yourself anyway, and you can ensure that they don't clash with a day where you need to do lots of communal eating, such as a party or family get together.

The 5:2 diet even allows for things not going quite to plan. If, for some reason, you get stuck in a situation where you can't avoid eating normal size portions – say, your boss insists on taking the team out for a pizza – then you can admit defeat and put off one of your two fasting days to later in the week.

And that's what makes the 5:2 diet so popular: it puts you in control. And, as you're the one steering your own progress, you are much more likely to keep to it and lose those pounds you're longing to wave goodbye to!

Health benefits

You only have to lose a few pounds to recognise that shifting that excess fat can work wonders for your physical and mental health. Your clothes feel looser, your skin looks brighter and somehow you feel you can cope so much better with whatever life has to throw at you.

Getting to within your normal weight range offers many more benefits than just being able to fit into your old jeans.

There are also many general benefits associated with losing excess weight. If you're overweight or obese, you have a higher risk of such health conditions as:

- High blood pressure
- Heart disease
- Stroke
- Type 2 diabetes
- Some types of cancer
- Infertility
- Osteoarthritis
- Back pain
- Depression

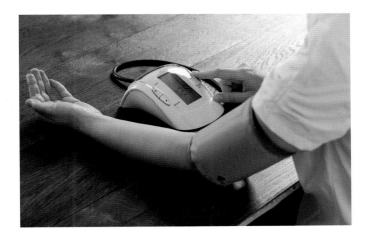

Getting your weight back down to an acceptable level can help reduce the risks of developing many of the above conditions.

What is my ideal weight?

You can get five people of the same height together and they will all look different. There will be people with broad shoulders and others with tiny frames. That's why standard height/ weight charts allow a fair few pounds of leeway. What's an ideal weight for one person might be way too low (or too high) for another.

GPs often use BMI as an indicator as to whether your weight falls into an acceptable category. BMI stands for Body Mass Index and is a simple mathematical device that can quickly establish if you are an appropriate weight.

It works as an excellent guide for most people. Others who have a very high proportion of lean muscle, such as rugby players and serious athletes, may find that their BMI makes them appear fatter as more of their body weight is muscle and not fat.

For your average office worker or parent, BMI is a good way of finding out if your weight is within a healthy range. Broadly speaking, if your BMI comes out at 25 or over, you're overweight. If it's over 30, you're classified as obese.

Use a calculator to work out your BMI. Weigh yourself in kilograms (kg) then divide your weight by your height in metres (m). Divide the answer by your height again to get your correct BMI. E.g: if you are 1.65 metres tall and weigh 75 kg, the sum would be as follows:

- 75 divided by 1.65 = 45.45

- Now divide by your height again: 45.45 divided by 1.65 = 27.54

- 27.54 is your BMI which would put you into the overweight category.

Using fasting as a weight loss regime in the 21st century is recognised to have a range of benefits. These include: loss of excess weight; flushing toxins out of the body; cleansing the digestive system; clearing the mind; gaining energy; and allowing the body time to rest and recover.

Many people who have tried the 5:2 diet sing its praises for the fact that severely restricting calories two days a week is actually quite manageable. And that is quite simply because your brain fully understands that it's for a very short space of time before 'normal' eating is resumed. It's a bit like waiting for a big birthday bash or counting the days down to Christmas. You know the end is in sight so that in itself makes whatever you're doing much more workable. And like dieting, if you can keep to the regime, you're bound to get results.

Another benefit is that you're less likely to crash and burn due to weeks and weeks of what you perceive to be daily deprivation. Because only two days are restricted, and the other five days of the week are not, it puts you in a psychologically stronger place to keep going.

And when you've reached your desired weight, using the 5:2 theory means that it's easy to go back on the diet if you slip up and gain a few pounds. You'll have already programmed your brain to accept this way of eating, so it can become a lifestyle choice, if that's what you want.

Is it safe?

Even if you are in good general health and think you'll be fine to do the 5:2 diet, it's always a good idea to check with your GP first.

You shouldn't embark on this plan if:

- You are a child or teenager

- You are pregnant

- You are breast-feeding

- You have a history of eating disorders.

If you have type 2 diabetes or a lowered immune system, this diet might be right for you but you MUST check first with your doctor.

Before you start, stick a picture of yourself as you are now in this space – then in a few weeks' time, you'll notice the difference!

It's also a good idea to take your measurements. Sometimes, even if the weight loss appears to be slow, you'll be losing those vital inches or centimetres.

Measurements now:

Bust/Chest

Waist

Hips

How to use this book

This book has been devised to help you stick to the 5:2 diet by offering lots of practical advice, recipe suggestions and handy hints.

Exactly how you choose to use your restricted calories on fast days (500 for women or 600 for men) is entirely up to you. The more you can personalise your day's eating, the better your chance of success.

That's why we've come up with a selection of recipes for breakfasts, lunches, main meals, desserts and treats.

The best laid plans

Everyone knows that no two days are quite the same. No matter how you might plan, things might not go in exactly the way you expected to. That's one of the advantages of the 5:2 diet – if, for some reason, it becomes clear that your fasting day isn't working, don't worry! Go back to your normal eating plan and pick another day to fast.

How will I feel?

500 calories for women or 600 for men is obviously quite a severe restriction on what you would normally eat, but most people say they find it relatively easy to manage.

When you first start the 5:2 diet, you will probably get a few hunger pangs as your body adjusts. Occasionally, people might get a mild headache or the occasional bout of feeling dizzy. If this happens to you, take things steadily and don't over-exert yourself.

Ensure you drink plenty of liquids so that you keep hydrated.

Which days do I choose?

That's entirely up to you, but you need to leave at least one day between your two fasting days. If you try and fast two days on the trot, this way of eating can start to feel like deprivation. And feelings of deprivation can lead you to throwing in the towel and heading for the pizza menu.

Your own weekly schedule is the best guide. Many people like to choose Monday as a fasting day (after a bit of weekend indulgence) and then Thursday, but whatever's right for you is the answer.

You won't necessarily choose the same two fasting days each week either. For example, if you know you have a birthday celebration to attend, or a particularly stressful meeting on the cards, simply don't fast on those days.

what to eat and when

The 5:2 diet is just about the most tailor-made diet there is. You choose what you eat and when you eat it. On those two fasting days, the only real rules you follow are your own.

Fast days

On each fast day, women are allowed 500 calories and men can have 600 calories. You want those calories to offer you a good range of nutrients and be filling enough to get you through to the next day.

It can be tempting to go out and buy a 500-calorie bar of chocolate and be done with it. But there's no need to do that – that's the advantage of 5:2. There's no need to feel deprived when you know you can eat normally again tomorrow.

On the 5:2 diet, you need to look quite carefully at the foods you choose to eat on the fasting days. Picking sensibly can reduce feelings of hunger and ensure that you get to the end of the day without cracking and diving for the biscuit tin.

Some people choose to have their entire calorie allowance in one meal. While that is possible, it does also require a lot of willpower. You could have a hearty breakfast of 500 calories that keeps you going all day, but then what do you do when you hit a hard hunger attack 10 hours later and have no calories left?

Those iron-willed individuals like to wait as long as possible to eat, surviving on calorie-free drinks all day until they have a main meal in the early evening. Again, it can be tough to go so long without eating at all.

One of the best options is to split your calorie allowance, starting with a small breakfast, brunch or lunch, and then having the rest of your calories in the evening. Eating late afternoon or evening can give you a feeling of satisfaction and prevent the chance of you waking up with hunger pangs during the night.

Non-fast days

Treat these as ordinary eating days and aim to eat no more than the recommended daily allowance of 2000 calories for women or 2500 for men. You may think you're going to want to eat lots after a fast day, but you will probably find that you're actually more thoughtful and considered about what you eat.

Choose plenty of wholegrain cereals, fresh fruit and vegetables, lean meat and calcium rich products such as low-fat cheese and semi-skimmed milk.

How to fast

Which days do I fast?

The days you fast are entirely up to you. Just make sure that you don't fast for two days in a row. Many people like to choose Monday and then pick another day that suits them. Try to choose days when there aren't too many demands placed on you. For example, don't fast on a day when you have a 200-mile drive ahead or a job interview. Ideally, fast days should be days where there is nothing unusual planned – just a simple, calm, straightforward day.

When do I eat on my fast days?

Really, it's up to you! Maybe you don't care to eat much in the evening. If so, you may be best to eat most of your calories at lunch. Or, if you can't get out of bed without breakfast to tempt you, then have something much earlier in the day.

Over the next few pages, there are plenty of ideas for meals to tempt your taste buds. You might find it best to try some of these as you get used to your new way of eating, but there are bound to be favourites of your own you're going to want to include in your fast day plans.

Some people choose to eat a small breakfast and then stick to plenty of low-calorie drinks, such as water, tea and coffee throughout the day, saving up most of their calories for an evening meal.

Others find that they can happily manage without breakfast – relying on low-calorie drinks – until much later on in the morning. Then they might have a light snack followed by something a little more filling later on.

The following recipe ideas will give you plenty of inspiration about what to eat and when. Remember, it may take a few fast days for you to work out what's right for you.

Splitting the days

Make sure your two fast days are spread over the week and not back-to-back. The aim of the 5:2 diet is that your two fast days are intermingled between standard eating days – not squashed together. You don't have to stick to the same two days each week. Just pick the days that are best for you.

Keep a record

When taking part in a weight loss regime, it's always a good idea to keep a record of what you've eaten and when. Even better, keep a note of your mood at the time as this can often pin-point times when you want to eat simply because you're bored or fed up. The diary pages further on in this book will help you keep track.

Stay busy

There are going to be times on fast days when you will feel peckish and have already used up your daily calorie allowance. One of the best things to do when hunger strikes is to do something to take your mind off it.

- Take a warm bubble bath.
- Start a new project – treat yourself to some wool and get knitting or find a new game on your phone or tablet to enjoy. Anything that keeps your fingers busy is great.
- Try painting watercolours.
- Have a clear out of your bedroom cupboards. De-cluttering is great for the mood and makes the time fly.
- Treat yourself to a magazine – not one that's crammed with pictures of cake though!
- Go for a long stroll with or without the dog.
- Have a long catch-up with a friend you've not seen for ages.
- Go to bed a bit earlier and take a good book with you.

Early days

As with anything new, the early days of a new diet regime can be the toughest. This is the time when you have to get used to a new way of eating, and there will be times when you feel uncertain or unsure about whether you're eating the right thing at the right time.

You'll also probably be feeling pretty happy right now – at your decision to lose weight and about the fact that there are plenty of lovely dishes to enjoy on fast days. And even better, the fact that you know that if you stick to your calorie limits on two days, you can relax on the other five!

How to eat

No point beating about the bush – on fast days, you're not going to eat much at all. That is why it's really important to eat food you enjoy. Don't pick meals containing ingredients you hate. For example, if you've always loathed cottage cheese, there's no point in adding it to your fast day. Eating stuff you dislike is only going to make you want to throw in the towel!

Follow these tips for maximum success:

• On fast days, ensure your meals include some protein as protein-rich foods can help to keep you feeling satisfied for longer. Protein foods include fish, lean meats and poultry, eggs, low-fat milk and cheese.

• Weigh and measure everything.

• Take a multi-vitamin supplement to make sure you're not missing out on essential vitamins.

• Add leafy vegetables to your fast days– try cabbage, kale and spring greens or go for salad vegetables like rocket, fresh spinach and lamb's lettuce. Adding extra low-calorie vegetables like these can help keep you full and add vital fibre to your day.

- Make salad foods your friend. Not only does salad add lots of fibre but it also makes small meals look bigger and more colourful. Try grating carrot and mixing with rocket and red pepper for a real traffic light of a side dish!

- Drink plenty. Fresh water is best. Add a squeeze of fresh lemon for extra zing. Other low-calorie drinks include tea, coffee and herbal teas.

- Cook in a non-stick pan to avoid having to use fat. Add a little water if need be.

- Use skimmed milk and very low-fat yogurt options.

- Avoid alcohol on fast days. Alcohol supplies empty calories and, when you're restricted, you want to use them all for food.

- Add spices to your food – they tempt the taste buds, make food more enjoyable and give meals a kick.

- Add fresh herbs – a few torn basil leaves, or a sprinkle of chopped coriander add a zesty zing to any dish.

- Use a smaller plate than normal – it tricks your brain into thinking you're eating more!

Make an occasion

Just because you're limited to 500 or 600 calories on two days of the week, this doesn't mean you should scoff standing up.

Make an occasion of every mouthful. Set the table with proper place mats. Pour a long cool glass of water and add a slice of lemon or lime for extra pizzazz. Use proper linen napkins. Turn off the radio or television and make eating a real event. One of the reasons that many of us gain weight in the first place is that we eat without really noticing what we're putting into our mouths.

Use your fast days to really get re-acquainted with food. Savour the texture, the taste, admire the wonderful colours on your plate and really enjoy them.

Eating with others

It certainly demands more willpower if you are eating with others on your fast days. You need a couple of weapons in your armoury – be firm if they try to tempt you, and explain calmly how much better you're feeling as a result of your 5:2 plan.

If you find it really hard to stay focused – especially if you're cooking for others – you might like to eat your own meal first. This allows you peace and quiet to concentrate and it also stops you picking and tasting as you cook. And it's only for a couple of days of the week – that very fact means that people around you are likely to be much more tolerant of your fast days.

Seasonal changes

We all change what we eat depending on the weather so let the seasons be your guide when it comes to the 5:2 diet. If it's warm outside, opt for plenty of colourful salads and long cool drinks. Eat al fresco if you can – being out in the sunshine works wonders for your mood. If it's chilly, steam cabbage and broccoli to add to your plate, or make hearty soups using low-calorie tinned tomatoes and passata as your base.

Motivation and goal setting

What's your motivation?

Any actress will tell you that, in order to understand the character they are playing, they need to know why she's doing what she's doing. In other words, what's her motivation? The same goes for anyone on the 5:2 diet.

You need to know why you're doing it – and what you aim to get out of it. Research shows that people who have a clear goal in life are generally more likely to succeed. In other words, if you have a clear idea of exactly what you want, you're more likely to achieve it.

So, before you start this new way of eating, take a little time to consider why you're going on the 5:2 diet and what your goals are.

Most of us have both long-term and short-term goals. It's a good idea to have something close to aim for as well as something much further away. It means that you always have something new to work towards and achieve.

Short term

Short-term goals can be anything you like.

For example, you may want to shed a few pounds simply to get back into your jeans, or to get back to your usual weight after a particularly indulgent holiday. You may have a big event on the horizon, a wedding or birthday bash. Maybe you've decided that all this extra weight isn't good for your health and you want to get yourself in shape. You could even be combining the 5:2 diet with a training plan for a fun run, or even a half marathon.

Don't consign resolutions to the New Year. Plans for a new you can start any time!

Long term

Just as it sounds, long-term goals are over-arching – they span a longer period and take more time to achieve. For you, it could be that you want weight loss to be part of a whole new life plan, a new direction you see yourself going in. Maybe you plan a career change soon and want to feel more confident about the way you look.

Perhaps you want to increase your overall health and know that being at the right weight for your height is all part of the process.

Take time

Whatever your aims, give yourself time and patience to get there. And with determination, you'll succeed!

Reward yourself

Everyone likes a little pat on the back and, when you're trying to lose weight, it's even more important that you tell yourself 'well done' as you head towards your goal.

It doesn't have to be a big gesture and it doesn't even need to cost much money. But do remember to treat yourself every time you reach a milestone. Whether you want to lose five pounds or five stone, take baby steps and reward yourself along the way.

Try some of these:

- **A star chart.** It works wonders for children, why not try it for yourself? Every time you lose a pound, give yourself a sticker. Then say, when you lose five pounds, you can 'cash' that in for a little low-cost reward, such as a new magazine, or a fun pair of socks.

- **A pebble jar.** Get an empty jar, and every time you lose a pound, put a pebble in it. Watch the jar fill up as you lose weight.

- **A weight bag.** Get yourself a 'bag for life' and every time you lose a pound, find a household item that weighs roughly the same. You'll be amazed just how much weight you've lost every time you pick up the bag. And think how much more energetic you'll feel without those extra pounds hanging on to your hips!

- **Chart it!** Draw yourself a graph and map your progress. This can be really useful on difficult weeks. If you see the graph spike upwards when you have a challenging week or two, it can give you the motivation to focus and get that line heading south.

- **Save it!** On your fast days, as you're only going to be eating 500 or 600 calories, there's a good chance you'll be saving money. Work out what your usual daily meals would have cost and pop the coins you've saved in a special piggy bank. At the end of the diet, tip them out and treat yourself.

Being active

Now is the time to get active. We're constantly being told that we're a nation of couch potatoes so it's wise to incorporate exercise into all areas of your life. Our sedentary lives, working at computers and watching television, can lead to weight gain. And, once we've got used to sitting around so much, it can be hard to push ourselves to get moving.

If catching up with the soaps or sitting down with a good book is one of your favourite pastimes, don't worry. You don't have to give it up. Instead, it's a good idea to try and incorporate exercise into your daily life.

If that thought makes you groan, don't despair. If you're one of those people who hated gym lessons as a kid, it's not the end of the world. You don't have to rush out and take up a sport you loathe.

It's all about keeping moving and making activity an integral part of every day. Start simply – walk about while you talk on the phone, get up and do a few stretches every 20 minutes or so if you're tied to a computer during your working day. If you take usually take the lift, then choose the stairs instead. It might seem tough to begin with, but it will get easier every day.

Why exercise?

Making the effort to keep active every day helps keep your heart healthy, reduces your risk of serious illness and strengthens muscles and bones.

It can help give you better results while you're dieting too - helping your weight loss and toning up muscles as well. It also means you're more likely to keep to your desired weight, even after you stop doing the 5:2 diet.

If you're new to regular exercise or have any specific health conditions, do ensure you consult your GP first before taking up any kind of fitness regime.

Timetable it

You don't have to set certain times aside for exercise – just add it into your everyday timetable. For example, if you get the bus to work, get off two or three stops earlier and walk the rest of the way. If you're going shopping, park the car at the very far end of the supermarket. Do you normally just nip the dog around the block? Then make time for a longer walk. Post those letters at another post box rather than the one on the corner.

Fit it in

Make ordinary chores more energetic. Not only will you get better results around the house, but you will start to feel fitter too. Really put some elbow grease into cleaning those windows or be really vigorous when you're mopping the kitchen floor. Pop some high energy music on when you're hoovering – not only will it boost your mood, but you'll find you move more too.

On the cheap

There are plenty of ways to boost your activity levels without spending much at all (if anything). Think about your surroundings, where you live and where you work or spend lots of time. How could you incorporate these locations into your daily life more frequently?

Try the following ideas:

- The great outdoors is just beyond the door. Step out and gradually build up your speed and the distance you go each day. It doesn't matter whether you live in a town or a tiny village – there are plenty of places to walk. Get more acquainted with your locality. Even if you live in an inner city or bustling town, take time to stride out. You'll be amazed how good it makes you feel. And you'll spot all kinds of things you miss when you're driving – urban architecture, interesting shops, pretty plants and beautiful birds.

- Dog walk. If you haven't got one, there's bound to be a friend or neighbour who is happy to lend you their dog for an extra walk. This is a great way to keep yourself moving, as dogs can often get very excited at the prospect of a walk and will keep you at a steady walking pace.

- If you have children, get them walking with you. They might moan, but offer them non-food incentives. By taking them with you, you're setting a fantastic example and encouraging the whole family to become more active and excited about keeping fit and healthy.

- Most leisure centres offer low-cost swim times. Swimming is a great form of exercise, whatever your shape. Because it's non-weight bearing, it places less pressure on the joints. Have an early morning swim to set you up for the day or an evening swim which can lead to a great night's sleep.

- Call a friend who you haven't recently spoken to or seen for a few weeks and invite them for a long walk around the local park or town. You will be chatting away and probably won't even realise how much fantastic exercise you're getting.

- Dance away. Pop on the radio or your portable music player and off you go. Dance around the kitchen, hula hula through the hall and waltz around the living room. Again, dance is one of those activities which is good for your mood as well as your body!

- Wash the car. Not just a cursory wipe. Get a big bucket full of car shampoo and scrub away. After washing it, try polishing it too, to really get your arms working. The benefit means you have a super sparkly vehicle and you're burning calories too.

Breakfasts

If you are trying to restrict your calorie intake, it can be very tempting to skip breakfast. As long as your diet allows it, you should always make the effort to eat a nutritious, filling breakfast. If you start the day with the right foods, you will fuel yourself with long-lasting energy.

If you ate your last meal over 12 hours ago, you will probably want to include a breakfast option on your fasting days. Eating breakfast peps up your metabolism, gives you energy and prepares you for the day ahead.

The following recipes will provide you with the inspiration you need to create a delicious, low-calorie breakfast. From Egg and Sausage Bake to the Lean Green Smoothie Bowl, there is a breakfast option for everyone.

Alternatively, if you decide against eating breakfast on a fasting day, because you want to make the most of your calories later in the day, at least make the effort to start your day with a glass of water mixed with a squeeze of lemon juice. This will provide you with essential, much-needed hydration.

MAKES: 4

Preparation time: **5 minutes**

Cooking time: **18 minutes**

Calories per egg: **277**

Avocado and bacon eggs

2 avocados, halved and stoned

4 medium eggs

2 rashers back bacon, thinly sliced

1 tbsp parsley, finely chopped

1. Preheat the oven to 220°C (200°C fan) / 425F / gas 7.
2. Enlarge the stone cavity of the avocados with a teaspoon to make space for the eggs.
3. Arrange the avocados cut side up in a snug baking dish and break an egg into the middle of each one.
4. Scatter over the bacon and season with salt and pepper, then bake for 18 minutes or until the egg whites have set, but the yolks are still a little runny.
5. Sprinkle with parsley and serve immediately.

SERVES: 4

Preparation time: **5 minutes**
Calories per portion: **191**

Breakfast fruit salad

3 nectarines, stoned and cut into wedges

1 kiwi fruit, peeled, quartered and sliced

12 strawberries, quartered

25 g / 1 oz / ¾ cup sorrel leaves

100 g / 3 ½ oz / ½ cup fresh goat's curd

50 g / 1 ¾ oz / ½ cup toasted oats

1 tbsp runny honey

2 tbsp apple juice

1. Divide the nectarines, kiwi fruit, strawberries and sorrel leaves between four bowls.

2. Break the goat's curd into small pieces and scatter over the top, then sprinkle with toasted oats.

3. Dissolve the honey in the apple juice, then drizzle it over the top and serve.

MAKES: 2

Preparation time: **15 minutes**
Calories per portion: **147**

Ombre strawberry smoothie

2 tbsp maple syrup

250 ml / 9 fl. oz / 1 cup buttermilk

150 g / 5 ½ oz / 1 cup strawberries

75 ml / 2 ½ fl. oz / ⅓ cup orange juice

½ tsp stevia

mint sprigs, to garnish

1. Stir the maple syrup into the buttermilk and divide between two glasses.

2. Put the strawberries in a liquidizer with the orange juice and stevia and blend until smooth.

3. Pour two thirds of the strawberry smoothie over the back of a spoon into the glasses, then swirl very gently with a skewer.

4. Pour the rest of the strawberry smoothie over the back of the spoon to float it on top.

5. Garnish with mint and serve.

SERVES: 2

Preparation time: **5 minutes**

Cooking time: **4 minutes**

Calories per portion: **528**

Avocado and egg on rye

2 large eggs

2 slices rye bread

1 ripe avocado, peeled and stoned

50 g / 1 ¾ oz / ⅓ cup low-fat feta, crumbled

50 g / 1 ¾ oz / ¼ cup low-fat cream cheese

2 red spring onions (scallions), finely chopped, red and green parts separated

½ lime, cut into wedges

1. Poach the eggs in lightly simmering water for 4 minutes or until cooked to your liking.

2. Meanwhile, toast the rye bread.

3. While the bread is toasting, mash together the avocado, feta and cream cheese. Stir in the red part of the spring onions and squeeze in two of the lime wedges, then season to taste with salt and pepper.

4. Spread the avocado mixture onto the toast and top with the poached eggs. Scatter over the spring onion greens, sprinkle with pepper and garnish with the rest of the lime wedges.

SERVES : 1

Preparation time: **5 minutes**
Cooking time: **15 minutes**
Calories per portion: **431**

Egg and sausage bake

2 medium eggs

1 frankfurter sausage, sliced

50 g / 1 ¾ oz / ⅓ cup reduced-fat smoked
pork sausage, sliced

1 slice white bread

1 tsp parsley, finely chopped

1. Preheat the oven to 180°C (160°C fan) / 350F /
   gas 4.

2. Break the eggs into a round baking dish
   and scatter over the frankfurter and
   pork sausage.

3. Transfer to the oven and bake for 15 minutes
   or until the egg whites have set.

4. Meanwhile, toast the bread and cut it in half
   diagonally.

5. Sprinkle the eggs with parsley and serve with
   toast on the side.

SERVES: 2

Preparation time: **15 minutes**

Freezing time: **2 hours**

Calories per portion: **599**

Lean green smoothie bowl

2 bananas, sliced

2 kiwi fruit, sliced

100 g / 3 ½ oz / ⅔ cup green
   seedless grapes

35 g / 1 ¼ oz / 1 cup young kale, chopped

35 g / 1 ¼ oz / 1 cup baby leaf spinach

250 ml / 9 fl. oz / 1 cup soya milk

250 ml / 9 fl. oz / 1 cup apple juice

1 tbsp chia seeds

1 tbsp hulled hemp seeds

50 g / 1 ¾ oz / ½ cup granola

25 g whole almonds, sliced

1 tbsp pumpkin seeds

2 dried figs, sliced

4 strawberries, sliced

1. Spread out the banana, kiwi fruit and grapes on a greaseproof paper lined baking tray and freeze for at least 2 hours. The fruit can then be transferred to a freezer bag and stored for future use or used straight away.

2. Put the kale and spinach in a liquidizer with the coconut milk and apple juice. Blend until smooth.

3. Add the frozen fruit and blend again until smooth, then pour into two chilled bowls.

4. Sprinkle the chia and hemp seeds over two thirds of the bowl and sprinkle the granola over half of the bowl. Top with almonds, pumpkin seeds and figs. Garnish with strawberries and serve immediately.

SERVES : 8

Preparation time: **15 minutes**

Cooking time: **1 hour**

Calories per portion: **263**

Strawberry granola yogurt pots

1 tbsp olive oil

75 ml / 2 ½ fl. oz / ⅓ cup apple juice

75 ml / 2 ½ fl. oz / ⅓ cup agave nectar

100 g / 3 ½ oz / 1 cup rolled porridge oats

75 g / 2 ½ oz / ¾ cup barley flakes

50 g / 1 ¾ oz / ½ cup walnuts, chopped

25 g sunflower seeds

25 g mixed candied peel, chopped

800 ml / 1 pint 7 oz / 3 ¼ cups 0% fat
   Greek yogurt

200 g / 7 oz / 1 ⅓ cups strawberries,
   halved or quartered if large

2 tbsp chia seeds

1. Preheat the oven to 160°C (140°C fan) / 325F /
   gas 3.

2. Stir the oil, apple juice and agave nectar
   together in a bowl with a pinch of salt then
   toss it with the oats, barley flakes, walnuts,
   sunflower seeds and candied peel.

3. Spread out the mixture on a large baking
   tray and bake for 1 hour, stirring every
   10 minutes to ensure it all toasts evenly.
   Leave the granola to cool completely,
   then store in an airtight jar.

4. When you're ready to serve, spoon half of
   the granola into eight glasses and top with
   yogurt. Sprinkle with the rest of the granola
   and top with strawberries and chia seeds.

MAKES : 350 ML

Preparation time: **15 minutes**
Calories per 350 ml: **119**

Pineapple and lime juice

1 pineapple, peeled and cut into chunks

1 lime, cut into chunks

1. Process the pineapple and lime through an electronic juicer, according to the manufacturer's instructions.

2. Pour the juice over ice to chill and serve immediately.

SERVES : 6

Preparation time: **15 minutes**

Cooking time: **1 hour**

Chilling time: **4 hours**

Calories per portion: **433**

Buckwheat granola and chia pots

50 ml / 1 ¾ fl. oz / ¼ cup runny honey

600 ml / 1 pint / 2 ½ cups soya milk

100 g / 3 ½ oz / ½ cup chia seeds

75 ml / 2 ½ fl. oz / ⅓ cup maple syrup

75 ml / 2 ½ fl. oz / ⅓ cup apple juice

1 tbsp extra virgin olive oil

175 g / 6 oz / 1 ¾ cups rolled
buckwheat flakes

100 g / 3 ½ oz / ¾ cup walnuts, chopped

150 g / 5 ½ oz / 1 cup mixed berries,
chopped if large

1 vanilla pod, cut into 6 pieces

1. Dissolve the honey in the soya milk, then stir
   in the chia seeds. Cover and chill in the fridge
   for 4 hours or ideally overnight.

2. Preheat the oven to 160°C (140°C fan) / 325F /
   gas 3.

3. Stir the maple syrup, apple juice and oil
   together in a bowl with a pinch of salt
   then toss it with the buckwheat flakes
   and walnuts.

4. Spread out the mixture on a large baking
   tray and bake for 1 hour, stirring every
   10 minutes to ensure it all toasts evenly.
   Leave the granola to cool completely,
   then store in an airtight jar.

5. When you're ready to serve, spoon a little
   granola into the bottom of six small glasses
   or jars. Stir the chia mixture and spoon it on
   top, then add a little more granola.

6. Top with berries and garnish with a piece of
   vanilla pod.

SERVES: 6

Preparation time: **15 minutes**

Cooking time: **1 hour**

Calories per portion: **355**

Granola with yogurt and blueberries

75 ml / 2 ½ fl. oz / ⅓ cup maple syrup

75 ml / 2 ½ fl. oz / ⅓ cup apple juice

1 tbsp extra virgin olive oil

175 g / 6 oz / 1 ¾ cups rolled porridge oats

100 g / 3 ½ oz / ¾ cup hazelnuts, chopped

600 ml / 1 pint / 2 ½ cups 0% fat
  Greek yogurt

150 g / 5 ½ oz / 1 cup blueberries

6 strawberries, cut into a fan

1. Preheat the oven to 160°C (140°C fan) / 325F / gas 3.
2. Stir the maple syrup, apple juice and oil together in a bowl with a pinch of salt then toss it with the oats and hazelnuts.
3. Spread out the mixture on a large baking tray and bake for 1 hour, stirring every 10 minutes to ensure it all toasts evenly.
4. Leave the granola to cool completely, then store in an airtight jar.
5. When you're ready to serve, spoon three quarters of the granola into six glass goblets and top with yogurt. Shake over the rest of the granola and arrange the blueberries on top.
6. Garnish each one with a fan-cut strawberry.

Light bites and lunches

It is all too easy to grab a hot lunch from drive-thru fast food restaurants or to choose a high-calorie sandwich from a local supermarket. Make the effort to avoid this, as these options will not help you keep within your calorie intake limits on fasting days.

The light bites and lunches in this chapter are ideal for keeping your energy levels up without consuming too many calories at once.

Many of the following light bites and lunch recipes are portable too, making it easy to take lunch with you when you're at work or on the go. The recipes in this chapter are easy-to-follow and low in calories.

The soups and salads are perfect for getting your daily quota of vegetables and vitamins. It is a great idea to make a big batch of soup or salad, which you can then split up into individual portions. This will save you money and make it really convenient for you to just grab a portion of soup or salad before you walk out of the door.

Alternatively, the Mushroom and Cheese Bruschetta or Smoked Salmon Ciabatta are filling and packed with flavour.

MAKES: 10

Preparation time: **5 minutes**

Cooking time: **5 minutes**

Calories per portion: **150**

Mushroom and cheese bruschetta

1 baguette, cut into 10 slices

150 g / 5 ½ oz Romano,
    cut into 10 slices

½ leek, thinly sliced

5 closed cap mushrooms, thickly sliced

1 tsp dried oregano

½ tsp dried chilli (chili) flakes

dill and flat-leaf parsley, to garnish

1. Toast one side of the baguette slices under a hot grill.

2. Turn them over and top each one with a slice of Romano and some of the leek and mushrooms. Sprinkle with oregano, chilli, salt and pepper.

3. Grill for 3 minutes or until the mushrooms are cooked and the cheese has started to melt underneath.

4. Serve immediately.

MAKES: 6

Preparation time: **1 hour**

Cooking time: **45 minutes**

Calories per portion: **352**

Lamb, dill and tomato turnovers

400 g / 14 oz / 2 ²/₃ cups strong white bread flour, plus extra for dusting

1 tsp easy blend dried yeast

1 tsp fine sea salt

1 tbsp olive oil

300 g / 10 ½ oz / 2 cups boneless lamb neck, cut into 1 cm pieces

1 shallot, finely chopped

1 clove of garlic, crushed

3 medium tomatoes, peeled, deseeded and diced

1 small bunch dill, finely chopped

1 large egg, beaten

1 tbsp sesame seeds

1. Mix together the flour, yeast and salt and stir the oil into 280 ml of warm water. Stir the liquid into the dry ingredients then knead on a lightly oiled surface for 10 minutes or until smooth and elastic.

2. Leave the dough to rest covered with oiled clingfilm for 1–2 hours or until doubled in size.

3. Preheat the oven to 190°C (170°C fan) / 375F / gas 5 and grease a large non-stick baking tray.

4. Knead the dough for 2 more minutes then roll it out into a large rectangle and cut into six squares.

5. Mix the lamb with the shallot, garlic, tomatoes and dill and season with salt and pepper. Divide the mixture between the dough squares, then fold them in half and crimp to seal.

6. Transfer to the baking tray, brush with egg and sprinkle with sesame seeds. Bake for 45 minutes or until cooked through and golden brown.

SERVES : 1

Preparation time: **5 minutes**
Calories per portion: **293**

Roquefort and pear salad

25 g / 1 oz / ¾ cup mixed baby salad leaves

1 ripe pear

50 g / 1 ¾ oz / ½ cup Roquefort, diced

1 tbsp pine nuts

1. Wash and spin the salad leaves, then arrange them on a plate.

2. Cut the pear in half and lay it on top, then scatter over the Roquefort and pine nuts.

3. Serve immediately.

SERVES: 4

Preparation time: **20 minutes**

Marinating time: **1 hour**

Cooking time: **10 minutes**

Calories per portion: **222**

Turkey and vegetable kebabs

2 tbsp maple syrup

2 tbsp lemon juice

½ tsp smoked paprika

½ tsp ground coriander

450 g / 1 lb / 3 cups turkey breast, cubed

4 sprigs rosemary, plus extra to garnish

1 courgette (zucchini), thickly sliced

1 yellow pepper, deseeded and cut
    into squares

1 red pepper, deseeded and cut into squares

1 red onion, cubed

1. Mix the maple syrup with the lemon juice, paprika and coriander and season with salt and pepper. Toss the mixture with the turkey and rosemary, then cover and marinate in the fridge for at least 2 hours.

2. Soak eight wooden skewers in cold water for 20 minutes.

3. Discard the rosemary and thread the turkey onto the skewers, alternating with the vegetables.

4. Cook the kebabs under a hot grill for 10 minutes, turning regularly, until cooked through.

5. Garnish with fresh rosemary sprigs, season with salt and pepper and serve immediately.

MAKES: 4

Preparation time: **5 minutes**

Cooking time: **5 minutes**

Calories per portion: **175**

Avocado and pine nut bruschetta

4 slices ciabatta

½ clove of garlic

1 avocado, peeled, stoned and diced

1 lemon, 1 slice taken and quartered,
   the rest juiced

1 tbsp pine nuts

1 handful rocket (arugula) leaves

1. Toast the ciabatta slices in a toaster or under
   a hot grill until golden and crisp.

2. Rub the ciabatta with the cut side of the
   garlic clove.

3. Toss the avocado with the lemon juice, pine
   nuts and rocket leaves and season with salt
   and pepper.

4. Pile the avocado mixture onto the bruschetta
   and garnish with the quartered lemon slice.

MAKES: 4

Preparation time: **1 hour**

Cooking time: **35 minutes**

Calories per portion: **409**

Courgette and leek tarts

2 cups boiling water

1 cup dried apricot, quartered

1 ½ cups orange juice

2 tbsp plain yogurt

1 tsp dark brown sugar

1. Preheat the oven to 200°C (180°C fan) / 400F / gas 6.
2. Rub the margarine into the flour and add just enough cold water to bind. Chill for 30 minutes then roll out and use to line four individual tart cases. Prick the pastry with a fork, line with clingfilm and fill with baking beans or rice.
3. Bake for 10 minutes then remove the clingfilm and baking beans and cook for another 5 minutes to crisp.
4. Lower the oven temperature to 150°C (130°C fan) / 300F / gas 2.
5. Whisk the eggs with the milk and half the cheese then divide it between the pastry cases. Arrange the courgette and leek on top and sprinkle with the rest of the cheese.
6. Bake the tarts for 20 minutes or until just set in the centre.
7. Garnish with dill and serve warm or at room temperature.

Preparation time: **2 hours 30 minutes**

Cooking time: **20 minutes**

Calories per portion: **207**

Rye and salad rolls

200 g / 7 oz / 1 ⅓ cups wholemeal rye flour, plus extra for sprinkling

200 g / 7 oz / 1 1⅓ cups malted granary flour

1 tsp easy blend dried yeast

1 tbsp brown sugar

1 tsp fine sea salt

1 tbsp olive oil

TO FILL

200 g / 7 oz / ⅔ cup reduced-fat hummus

50 g / 1 ¾ oz / 1 ½ cups mixed salad leaves

1 red onion, sliced

3 large tomatoes, sliced

1 cucumber, sliced

150 g / 5 ½ oz / 1 cup radishes, sliced

1 handful mustard cress

1. Mix together the flours, yeast, sugar and salt. Stir the oil into 280 ml of warm water then stir it into the dry ingredients.

2. Knead the mixture on an oiled surface with your hands for 10 minutes. Leave the dough to rest in a lightly oiled bowl, covered with oiled clingfilm, for 1–2 hours or until doubled in size.

3. Knead for 2 more minutes, then shape the dough into ten rolls. Transfer the rolls to a greased baking tray and cover with oiled clingfilm. Leave to prove for 1 hour or until doubled in size.

4. Meanwhile, preheat the oven to 220°C (200°C fan) / 425F / gas 7.

5. Sprinkle with a little more rye flour and bake for 20 minutes. Transfer to a wire rack and leave to cool completely.

6. Halve the rolls and spread the cut sides with hummus. Fill with salad and serve.

SERVES : 4

Preparation time: **10 minutes**

Cooking time: **1 hour 5 minutes**

Calories per portion: **293**

Pea soup

2 tbsp olive oil

1 onion, finely chopped

2 cloves of garlic, crushed

100 g / 3 ½ oz / ½ cup dried green split peas

1 litre / 1 pint 15 fl. oz / 4 cups
vegetable stock

300 g / 10 ½ oz / 2 cups garden peas,
podded weight

150 g / 5 ½ oz / 1 cup mangetout

parsley, to garnish

1. Heat half the oil in a saucepan and fry the onion for 10 minutes or until softened.

2. Add the garlic and split peas to the pan and cook for 2 more minutes, then stir in the vegetable stock.

3. Simmer for 45 minutes or until the split peas are starting to break down, then add the garden peas and mangetout. Simmer for 3 minutes or until tender, then remove a few of the peas and mangetout to use as a garnish.

4. Blend the soup until smooth with a liquidizer or immersion blender then taste and adjust the seasoning with salt and pepper.

5. Ladle into warm bowls and drizzle over the other tablespoon of olive oil.

6. Garnish with parsley and the reserved peas and mangetout, then serve immediately.

SERVES: 2

Preparation time: **5 minutes**

Cooking time: **15 minutes**

Calories per portion: **392**

Tomatoes with prawns and crab

16 cherry tomatoes

100 g / 3 ½ oz / ⅔ cup raw prawns (shrimp), peeled

2 tbsp white crab meat

1 tbsp olive oil

1 clove of garlic, crushed

1 tbsp flat-leaf parsley, chopped

50 g / 1 ¾ oz baguette (about ⅙)

1. Preheat the oven to 200°C (180°C fan) / 400F / gas 6.

2. Arrange the tomatoes in a snugly fitting baking dish. Bake for 10 minutes.

3. Meanwhile, mix the prawns and crab with the oil, garlic and parsley. Spoon the mixture over the tomatoes and return the dish to the oven for 5 minutes or until the prawns turn opaque.

4. Season with salt and pepper and serve immediately with a chunk of baguette.

SERVES : 1

Preparation time: **5 minutes**

Cooking time: **5 minutes**

Calories per portion: **158**

Tomato and basil bruschetta

2 slices ciabatta

2 tsp reduced-sugar sweet chilli sauce

2 tomatoes, diced

1 handful basil leaves, chopped

1. Toast the ciabatta slices in a toaster or under a hot grill until golden and crisp.

2. Spread the toast with chilli sauce.

3. Mix the tomatoes with the basil and season with salt and pepper, then pile the mixture onto the bruschetta.

SERVES: 2

Preparation time: **10 minutes**

Cooking time: **2 minutes**

Calories per portion: **383**

Cabbage, avocado and chickpeas

½ small savoy cabbage, chopped

200 g / 7 oz / 1 ⅓ cups canned chickpeas
   (drained weight)

1 avocado, peeled, stoned and diced

½ tsp stevia

¼ tsp ground cumin

1 lemon, half sliced, half juiced

1. Blanch the cabbage in boiling salted water
   for 2 minutes, then refresh in iced water
   and drain well.

2. Toss the cabbage with the chickpeas and
   avocado and arrange on two plates.

3. Stir the stevia and cumin into the lemon
   juice with a big pinch of salt, then drizzle
   it over the salads.

4. Garnish with sliced lemon and serve
   immediately.

SERVES: 4

Preparation time: **10 minutes**

Cooking time: **35 minutes**

Calories per portion: **280**

Butternut squash soup

2 tbsp olive oil

1 onion, finely chopped

2 cloves of garlic, finely chopped

1 ½ tsp dried oregano

1 ½ tsp dried chilli (chili) flakes

900 g / 2 lb / 1 large butternut squash, peeled, deseeded and cut into chunks

1 litre / 1 pint 15 fl. oz / 4 cups vegetable stock

75 ml / 2 ½ fl. oz / ⅓ cup 0% fat Greek yogurt

50 g / 1 ¾ oz / ½ cup pumpkin seeds

1. Heat the oil in a large saucepan and fry the onion and garlic for 10 minutes to soften without colouring.

2. Stir in 1 teaspoon each of the oregano and chilli flakes, then add the squash to the pan and stir to coat in the oil.

3. Pour in the stock and bring to the boil, then reduce the heat a little and simmer for 25 minutes or until the squash is tender.

4. Blend the soup until smooth, using a liquidizer or immersion blender, then taste and adjust the seasoning.

5. Ladle the soup into warm bowls and stir a little yogurt into the top of each one. Garnish with pumpkin seeds and the rest of the oregano and chilli flakes.

SERVES : 1

- Preparation time: **5 minutes**
  Calories per portion: **57**

Colourful salad

25 g mixed baby salad leaves

75 g / 2 ½ oz / ½ cup mixed red and yellow
  cherry tomatoes, halved

½ red pepper, sliced

50 g / 2 ½ oz / ⅓ cup radishes, sliced

50 g / 1 ¾ oz / ⅓ cup cucumber, halved
  and sliced

1 spring onion (scallion), chopped

1 small handful mixed herbs,
  roughly chopped

FOR THE DRESSING

½ tsp Dijon mustard

½ tsp runny honey

1 tbsp lemon juice

1. Toss the salad ingredients together and
   arrange on a plate.
2. Put all of the dressing ingredients in a small
   jar with a pinch of salt and pepper and shake
   well to emulsify.
3. Drizzle the dressing over the salad and
   serve immediately.

SERVES: 4

Preparation time: **10 minutes**

Cooking time: **40 minutes**

Calories per portion: **126**

Roasted sprouts with bacon

75 g / 2 ½ oz / ½ cup streaky bacon, chopped (approx. 4 rashers)

450 g / 1 lb / 3 ²/₃ cups Brussels sprouts, trimmed and halved

1 tbsp Parmesan, finely grated

1. Preheat the oven to 200°C (180°C fan) / 400F / gas 6.

2. Fry the bacon in a roasting tin for 3 minutes to release the fat. Remove the bacon from the pan with a slotted spoon and set aside.

3. Add the sprouts to the roasting tin and toss to coat in the fat. Season with salt and pepper.

4. Roast the sprouts for 35 minutes or until just tender. Add the bacon to the tin and return to the oven for 5 minutes.

5. Sprinkle the sprouts with Parmesan and serve immediately.

MAKES : 8

Preparation time: **35 minutes**
Calories per portion: **99**

Summer rolls

100 g / 3 ½ oz vermicelli rice noodles

8 rice paper wrappers

24 cooked king prawns, peeled

8 soft lettuce leaves

¼ cucumber, julienned

½ carrot, coarsely grated

2 tbsp light soy sauce

½ tsp sesame seeds

herbs and lime wedges, to garnish

1. Put the noodles in a bowl and pour over enough boiling water to cover by 5 cm (2 in). Leave to soak for 4 minutes, then drain well.

2. Dip the first rice paper wrapper in a bowl of cold water, then lay it out on a clean chopping board. Arrange three prawns across the middle, then lay a lettuce leaf on top and add some noodles, cucumber and carrot.

3. Fold over the sides of the wrapper, then roll it up to enclose the filling. Repeat with the rest of the ingredients to form eight rolls.

4. Stir the sesame seeds into the soy sauce and serve alongside for dipping.

5. Garnish with herbs and lime wedges.

SERVES: 4

Preparation time: **10 minutes**

Cooking time: **5 minutes**

Chilling time: **1 hour**

Calories per portion: **53**

Lightly pickled vegetable salad

100 ml / 3 ½ fl. oz / ½ cup rice wine vinegar

2 tbsp stevia

1 red chilli (chili), sliced

200 g / 7 oz / 1 ²/₃ cups carrot, spiralized or grated

150 g / 5 ½ oz / 1 ¼ cups radishes, thinly sliced

150 g / 5 ½ oz / 1 ¼ cups cucumber, thinly sliced

200 g / 7 oz / 1 ²/₃ cups red cabbage, finely shredded

100 g / 7 oz / 1 ²/₃ cups red onion, thinly sliced

4 lettuce leaves

fresh herbs, to garnish

1. Put the vinegar, stevia and chilli in a small saucepan with 75 ml of water and a pinch of salt. Bring to the boil, stirring occasionally.

2. Put the carrot, radishes and cucumber into three separate bowls and the cabbage and red onion into a fourth. Strain the vinegar mixture equally into each bowl and stir well.

3. Leave the vegetables to cool to room temperature, then cover and chill for at least 1 hour.

4. When you're ready to serve, drain the vegetables and layer them up inside four tall glass jars.

5. Top with lettuce and garnish with fresh herbs.

Preparation time: **15 minutes**

Cooking time: **15 minutes**

Chilling time: **2 hours**

Calories per portion: **284**

Crispy baked chicken bites

3 chicken breasts, sliced

150 ml / 5 ½ fl. oz / ⅔ cup buttermilk

2 tbsp light soy sauce

50 g / 1 ¾ oz / ½ cup fresh coconut, peeled and finely grated

75 g / 2 ½ oz / ½ cup panko breadcrumbs

1 tbsp black sesame seeds

lime wedges, salad and dark soy sauce, to serve

1. Mix the chicken with the buttermilk and soy sauce, then cover and chill for at least 2 hours.

2. Preheat the oven to 220°C (200°C fan) / 425F / gas 7 and line a large baking tray with greaseproof paper.

3. Mix the coconut, panko crumbs and sesame seeds in a wide shallow bowl. Wipe any excess marinade off the chicken, then roll to coat in the crumbs.

4. Spread out the chicken on the prepared baking tray and bake for 15 minutes, turning halfway through.

5. Serve immediately with soy sauce for dipping and lime wedges and salad on the side.

MAKES: 2

Preparation time: **5 minutes**
Calories per portion: **286**

Smoked salmon ciabatta

2 x 75 g / 2 ½ oz pieces ciabatta,
  halved horizontally

2 tbsp low-fat cream cheese

75 g / 2 ½ oz / ½ cup smoked salmon

50 g / 1 ¾ oz / ½ cup cucumber, sliced

1 large handful rocket (arugula)

1. Spread the ciabatta halves with cream cheese.
2. Fill the sandwiches with smoked salmon, cucumber and rocket.
3. Serve immediately.

Main meals

Main meals should be healthy, filling and delicious. From curries and burgers to stir-fries and pasta dishes, the following recipes will inspire you to cook exciting, varied main meals that you can enjoy time and time again.

A range of meat fits perfectly into the 5:2 diet, so long as you buy the leanest cuts of meat possible and remove all visible fat. If you choose poultry meat, ensure it is skinless too. Many supermarkets offer a range of meats with different fat percentages so always choose the lowest fat content available.

Lean meat and poultry offer essential proteins, which are even more important on fasting days. High protein foods can help you feel fuller for longer and supply vital ingredients such as iron.

The Baked Mediterranean Salmon dish is an ideal main meal. Fish is high in protein and many types of fish are low in calories. Always ensure that any fish you use is skinless. Some types of oily fish, such as salmon and tuna, are very high in essential oils.

Vegetables can be a fasting day's best buddy. They are high in fibre, packed with vitamins and minerals and are, therefore, very filling. A good serving of vegetables (steamed, roasted or otherwise) can go a long way in helping you feel full on your fasting days.

SERVES: 4

Preparation time: **20 minutes**

Cooking time: **35 minutes**

Calories per portion: **452**

Turkey meatball spaghetti

2 tbsp olive oil

2 shallots, finely chopped

1 clove of garlic, crushed

250 g / 9 oz / 1 ²/₃ cups minced turkey

50 g / 1 ¾ oz / ½ cup fresh brown breadcrumbs

1 large egg

200 ml / 7 fl. oz / ¾ cup tomato passata

200 ml / 7 fl. oz / ¾ cup chicken stock

250 g / 9 oz dried spaghetti

1 handful basil leaves

1. Heat half of the oil in a sauté pan and fry the shallots for 5 minutes or until softened. Add the garlic and cook for 2 more minutes, stirring constantly, then scrape the mixture into a mixing bowl and leave to cool.

2. Add the turkey, breadcrumbs and egg and mix well then shape into eight meatballs.

3. Heat the rest of the oil in the sauté pan and sear the meatballs on all sides.

4. Pour over the passata and stock and simmer gently for 20 minutes or until the meatballs are cooked all the way through. Season well with salt and pepper.

5. While the sauce is cooking, boil the pasta in salted water according to the packet instructions or until al dente.

6. Drain the pasta and stir it into the sauté pan, then tip everything onto a warm serving plate and garnish with basil.

SERVES : 4

Preparation time: **10 minutes**

Cooking time: **3 hours 30 minutes**

Calories per portion: **340**

Beef and vegetable stew

450 g / 1 lb / 3 cups lean braising steak, cut into large chunks

2 tbsp plain (all-purpose) flour

2 tbsp olive oil

1 onion, quartered and sliced

200 g / 7 oz / 1 ²/₃ cups carrots, sliced

200 g / 7 oz / 1 ²/₃ cups swede, cut into 1 cm dice

1 tsp sweet paprika

1 tbsp tomato puree

250 ml / 9 fl. oz / 1 cup tomato passata

500 ml / 17 ½ fl. oz / 2 cups beef stock

200 g / 7 oz / 1 ⅓ cups peas

parsley, to garnish

1. Season the braising steak with salt and pepper and dust all over with flour. Heat the oil in a wide cast iron casserole dish over a high heat. Sear the steak all over in batches, transferring the pieces to a plate when they are well coloured.

2. Add the onion, carrots and swede to the pan and fry for 10 minutes over a low heat, stirring regularly.

3. Stir in the paprika and tomato puree and cook for 1 minute. Stir in the passata and stock and return the beef to the pan.

4. Partially cover the pan with a lid and simmer gently for 3 hours or until the beef is tender and the sauce has reduced and thickened.

5. Add the peas and cook for 5 more minutes then season to taste with salt and pepper.

6. Garnish with parsley and serve.

SERVES : 4

Preparation time: **10 minutes**

Cooking time: **10 minutes**

Calories per portion: **328**

Chicken noodle stir-fry

400 g / 14 oz thin egg noodles

1 tbsp sunflower oil

1 tbsp fresh root ginger, finely chopped

3 large red chillies (chilies), sliced and
  deseeded if preferred

2 skinless chicken breasts, cubed

1 carrot, halved and very thinly sliced

1 courgette (zucchini), very thinly sliced

150 g / 5 ½ oz / 1 cup green beans,
  cut into short lengths

2 tbsp shaoxing rice wine

125 ml / 4 ½ fl. oz / ½ cup chicken stock

2 tbsp light soy sauce

1 tsp cornflour (cornstarch), slaked with
  1 tbsp cold water

2 tbsp flaked (slivered) almonds

1. Cook the noodles in boiling water according
   to the packet instructions or until al dente,
   then drain well.

2. Heat the oil in a large wok and fry the ginger
   and chillies for 2 minutes.

3. Add the chicken and stir-fry for 3 minutes or
   until lightly coloured. Add the carrot, courgette
   and beans and stir-fry for 2 minutes.

4. Add the rice wine, stock, soy sauce and
   noodles and stir-fry for 2 more minutes,
   then taste and adjust the seasoning with
   a little more soy sauce if needed.

5. Add the slaked cornflour and stir until the
   sauce thickens, then divide between four
   warm plates and serve sprinkled with
   flaked almonds.

SERVES: 4

Preparation time: **15 minutes**

Chilling time: **1 hour**

Cooking time: **8 minutes**

Calories per burger: **453**

Beetroot and chickpea burgers

125 g / 4 ½ oz / 1 cup raw beetroot, grated

150 g / 5 ½ oz / 1 cup canned chickpeas, drained

75 g / 2 ½ oz / ¾ cup low-fat feta cheese, crumbled

100 g / 3 ½ oz / 1 cup dried breadcrumbs

1 large egg

1 shallot, finely chopped

½ tsp ground coriander

1 tbsp olive oil

4 burger buns, halved horizontally

1 handful rocket (arugula)

1 tomato, sliced

2 radishes, sliced

50 g / 1 ¾ oz / ½ cup red cabbage, shredded

1. Put the beetroot, chickpeas, feta, breadcrumbs, egg, shallot and coriander in a food processor. Season with salt and pepper, then pulse until finely chopped and evenly mixed.

2. Shape the mixture into four patties, then chill in the fridge for 1 hour.

3. Heat the oil in a large frying pan and fry the burgers for 8 minutes, turning halfway through.

4. Top the bun bases with some of the rocket and the tomato and radishes. Lay a burger on top of each one.

5. Garnish with red cabbage and rocket and finish with the burger lids, then serve immediately.

SERVES: 2

Preparation time: **15 minutes**

Calories per portion: **370**

Raw asian salad

1 medium sized kohlrabi

4 spring onions

1 tsp sea salt flakes

1 nashi pear

1 Chinese white cabbage

a small bunch of coriander, roughly torn

25 g / 1 oz / 1/3 cup coconut flakes

1 tbsp fish sauce

1 tbsp rice wine vinegar

2 limes, juiced

1 tsp caster sugar

1 tsp black sesame seeds

1. Using a sharp knife or mandoline, shred the kohlrabi into thin strips. Fine chop the spring onions and add to a bowl with the shredded kohlrabi and the salt. Set aside for around 20 minutes to allow the salt draw out the moisture and soften the vegetables.

2. Peel and core the pear and thinly slice. Remove the core from the cabbage and thinly shred the leaves.

3. Combine the shredded vegetables in a clean bowl. Add the coriander and coconut.

4. Thoroughly mix the fish sauce, vinegar, lime juice, sugar and sesame seeds in a separate bowl until combined.

5. Pour the dressing over the salad and toss to coat before placing into serving bowls.

SERVES: 2

Preparation time: **10 minutes**
Cooking time: **40 minutes**
Calories per portion: **530**

Orange glazed chicken

1 orange, 2 slices taken, the rest juiced
25 g cranberries
2 chicken leg quarters (250 g / 9 oz each)
1 star anise
a few sprigs thyme
a few sprigs rosemary
2 tbsp marmalade

1. Preheat the oven to 200°C (180°C fan) / 400F / gas 6.
2. Arrange the orange slices and cranberries in a small roasting tin and lay the chicken on top. Season with salt and pepper, then scatter over the star anise, thyme and rosemary.
3. Transfer the tin to the oven and roast for 20 minutes.
4. Heat the orange juice with the marmalade and stir to dissolve, then pour it over the chicken and return to the oven for 20 minutes.
5. To test if the chicken is cooked, insert a skewer into the thickest part of the thigh. If the juices run clear, it is ready.
6. Serve the chicken immediately with vegetables.

SERVES: 4

Preparation time: **5 minutes**

Cooking time: **10 minutes**

Calories per portion: **179**

Thai green beef curry

1 tbsp coconut oil

2 tbsp Thai green curry paste

225 g / 8 oz / 1 ½ cups lean sirloin steak, cubed

100 g / 3 ½ oz / ²/₃ cup pea aubergines (eggplants)

12 Thai kermit aubergines (eggplants), halved

400 ml / 14 fl. oz / 1 ²/₃ cups beef stock

100 ml / 3 ½ fl. oz / ½ cup coconut milk

2 tbsp 0% fat Greek yogurt

1-2 tsp stevia sweetener

1-2 tbsp fish sauce

4 sprigs holy basil

1 red chilli (chili), sliced

1. Heat the oil in a wok and stir-fry the curry paste for 1 minute.

2. Add the steak and stir-fry until browned. Add both types of aubergine to the pan and turn to coat in the paste.

3. Stir in the stock and coconut milk then simmer for 5 minutes.

4. Take the pan off the heat and stir in the yogurt, 1 teaspoon of stevia and 1 tablespoon of fish sauce. Taste the curry and add more stevia or fish sauce if needed to get the perfect balance of sweet, salty and spicy.

5. Ladle into four warm bowls and serve garnished with holy basil and red chilli.

SERVES: 2

Preparation time: **45 minutes**

Cooking time: **30 minutes**

Calories per portion: **343**

Red rice aubergines

250 g / 9 oz / 1 ¼ cups red rice

500 ml / 17 ½ fl. oz / 2 cups vegetable stock

4 spring onions (scallions), chopped

1 yellow pepper, deseeded and diced

1 beefsteak tomato, deseeded and diced

2 small aubergines (eggplants),
    halved horizontally

1 tbsp olive oil

basil leaves to garnish

1. Put the rice and stock in a saucepan. Cover and simmer for 35 mins, stirring occasionally, until the rice is cooked al dente.

2. Preheat the oven to 180°C (160°C fan) / 350F / gas 4.

3. Stir the spring onions, peppers and tomato into the rice and season to taste with salt and pepper.

4. Arrange the aubergines cut-side-up in a roasting tin and spoon the rice mixture on top.

5. Drizzle with olive oil and bake for 30 minutes or until a skewer will slide easily into the centre of each aubergine.

6. Divide between two warm plates and garnish with basil.

SERVES : 1

Preparation time: **5 minutes**

Cooking time: **20 minutes**

Calories per portion: **354**

Baked mediterranean salmon

200 g / 7 oz portion salmon fillet

1 slice lemon

1 tsp thyme leaves

2 cherry tomatoes, halved

3 small stalks celery

½ bulb garlic

2 sprigs rosemary

1 bay leaf

1. Preheat the oven to 190°C (170°C fan) / 375F / gas 5.

2. Lay the salmon on a cast iron griddle and top with the lemon slice and thyme leaves. Season with salt and pepper then surround with the rest of the ingredients.

3. Bake the salmon for 20 minutes or until just turning opaque in the centre.

4. Serve hot or cold.

SERVES : 4

Preparation time: **15 minutes**

Cooking time: **20 minutes**

Calories per portion: **407**

Baked white bean burgers

400 g / 14 oz / 1 ²/₃ cups canned cannellini beans, drained

1 shallot, finely chopped

25 g / 1 oz / ¼ cup carrot, finely grated and squeezed of excess moisture

1 medium egg, lightly beaten

100 g / 3 ½ oz / 1 ⅓ cups fresh white breadcrumbs

4 white crusty rolls, approx. 70 g each

4 lettuce leaves

100 g / 3 ½ oz / ¾ cup pickled red cabbage, drained

1 tbsp mixed seeds, e.g.. linseeds, hulled hemp seeds, sesame seeds

cress, to garnish

1. Preheat the oven to 220°C (200°C fan) / 425F / gas 7 and line a large baking tray with greaseproof paper.

2. Mash the cannellini beans with a fork, then stir in the shallot, carrot, egg and half the breadcrumbs. Season with salt and pepper.

3. Shape the mixture into four patties, then coat them in the rest of the breadcrumbs.

4. Spread the patties out on the baking tray and bake for 20 minutes, turning halfway through.

5. Halve the rolls horizontally and lay a lettuce leaf on the base of each one. Top with the burgers and pickled cabbage, then sprinkle with seeds and garnish with cress.

6. Serve immediately.

SERVES: 4

Preparation time: **10 minutes**

Marinating time: **1 hour**

Cooking time: **45 minutes**

Calories per portion: **309**

Pork and vegetable bake

150 ml / 5 ½ fl. oz / ²/₃ cup pineapple juice

450 g / 1 lb / 3 cups lean pork, cubed

900 g / 2 lb / 1 large butternut squash, peeled, deseeded and cubed

2 tbsp olive oil

2 red peppers, deseeded and cubed

1 red onion, cut into wedges

1 tsp ground cumin

1 tsp ground coriander

1 tbsp flat-leaf parsley, finely chopped, plus extra to garnish

1 tbsp basil leaves, finely chopped, plus extra to garnish

1. Pour the pineapple juice over the pork and leave to marinate for 1 hour.

2. Preheat the oven to 200°C (180°C fan) / 400F / gas 6.

3. Arrange the squash in a single layer in a roasting tin and drizzle with oil. Season generously with salt and pepper and roast for 20 minutes.

4. Drain the pork, reserving the juice, and add it to the roasting tin with the peppers and onion. Stir the spices into the marinade and drizzle it over the top, then return the tin to the oven.

5. Roast for 25 minutes or until the pork is cooked through and the vegetables are tender.

6. Sprinkle with chopped parsley and basil and serve, garnished with a few extra sprigs of each herb.

MAKES : 6

Preparation time: **15 minutes**

Cooking time: **1 hour 15 minutes**

Calories per portion: **359**

Stuffed peppers

200 g / 7 oz / 1 cup brown lentils

2 tbsp olive oil

1 onion, finely chopped

1 tsp cumin seeds

2 cloves of garlic, finely chopped

175 g / 6 oz / ¾ cup basmati rice

½ tsp ground cinnamon

½ tsp paprika

150 g / 5 ½ oz / ²/₃ cup white-rinded goat's cheese, diced

6 peppers, tops sliced off and seeds removed

basil, to garnish

1. Put the lentils in a saucepan with enough cold water to cover by 2 ½ cm (1 in). Simmer for 15 minutes, then drain well.

2. Meanwhile, heat the oil in a saucepan and fry the onion and cumin over a low heat for 15 minutes. Add the garlic and cook for 5 minutes.

3. Add the rice, cinnamon and paprika and stir-fry until the rice sizzles. Stir in the lentils and 1 ½ teaspoons of salt, then pour in 600 ml water. When it boils, cover the pan, reduce the heat to its lowest setting and cook for 20 minutes. Turn off the heat and leave to stand, still covered, for 10 minutes.

4. Preheat the oven to 200°C (180°C fan) / 400F / gas 6.

5. Fold the goat's cheese carefully into the rice, then fill the peppers and put the tops back on.

6. Bake the peppers for 20 minutes or until tender to the point of a knife. Serve immediately, garnished with basil.

Desserts

Just because you're restricting your calorie intake, it should not mean that you skip dessert. The following desserts are easy to make and specify their calorie count, so that you can keep a track of your intake.

The following recipes in this chapter are delicious and tempting but still contain ingredients such as refined sugar. Because of this, you should make sure that you don't over-indulge on a daily basis. Instead, choose one of the desserts in this chapter as your weekend treat or mid-week reward for keeping to your calorie limits on fasting days. Having said this, some of the lower calorie desserts might be exactly what you need to get you through a fasting day.

From refreshing Pumpkin and Coconut Verrines to classic Crème Brûlée and Baked Apple, there is something to tempt everyone's sweet tooth in this chapter.

Be sure to check the calorie counts of these desserts – remember not to go over your calorie limit on fasting days.

SERVES : 8

Preparation time: **1 hour**

Cooking time: **1 hour**

Calories per portion: **378**

Plum cheesecake tart

100 g / 3 ½ oz / ½ cup low-fat
   margarine, cubed

200 g / 7 oz / 1 ⅓ cups wholemeal flour

600 g / 1 lb 5 oz / 2 ¾ cups low-fat
   cream cheese

150 ml / 5 fl. oz / ⅔ cup reduced-fat
   soured cream

50 g / 1 ¾ oz / ¼ cup stevia

2 large eggs, plus 1 egg yolk

2 tbsp plain (all-purpose) flour

6 plums, stoned and sliced

1. Preheat the oven to 200°C (180°C fan) / 400F /
   gas 6.

2. To make the pastry, rub the margarine into
   the flour and add just enough cold water to
   bind. Chill for 30 minutes then roll out on a
   floured surface and use to line a round tart dish.

3. Prick the pastry with a fork, line with
   clingfilm and fill with baking beans or rice.
   Bake for 10 minutes then remove the clingfilm
   and baking beans and cook for another
   8 minutes to crisp.

4. Reduce the oven temperature to 180°C (160°C
   fan) / 350F / gas 4.

5. Whisk together the cream cheese, soured
   cream, stevia, eggs and yolk and flour until
   smooth. Spoon the cheesecake mixture into
   the pastry case, then arrange the plums on top.

6. Bake the cheesecake for 40 minutes or until
   the centre is only just set. Leave to cool
   completely in the tin, then chill before serving.

MAKES : 16

Preparation time: **30 minutes**

Cooking time: **17 minutes**

Calories each: **179**

Chocolate toffee nut cookies

110 g / 4 oz / ½ cup brown sugar

50 g / 1 ¾ oz / ¼ cup caster (superfine) sugar

100 g / 3 ½ oz / ½ cup low-fat
    margarine, melted

1 tsp vanilla extract

1 medium egg

100 g / 3 ½ oz / ²/₃ cups wholemeal rye flour

25 g / 1 oz / ¼ cup unsweetened cocoa powder

FOR THE TOPPING

100 g / 3 ½ oz / ²/₃ cup sugar-free
    toffees, chopped

100 g / 3 ½ oz / ²/₃ cup roasted hazelnuts

50 g / 1 ¾ oz / ¹/₃ cup dark chocolate
    (min. 70% cocoa solids)

50 g / 1 ¾ fl. oz / ½ cup icing
    (confectioners') sugar

1. Preheat the oven to 160°C (140°C fan) / 325F / gas 3 and line two baking sheets with greaseproof paper.

2. Cream together the two sugars, margarine and vanilla extract until pale and well whipped then beat in the egg, followed by the flour and cocoa.

3. Drop tablespoons of the mixture onto the prepared trays, leaving plenty of room to spread.

4. Bake the cookies for 15 minutes or until the edges are starting to brown. Top with chopped toffee and hazelnuts and return to the oven for 2 minutes or until the toffee just starts to soften. Leave to cool completely.

5. Melt the chocolate in a microwave or bain-marie and drizzle it over the top.

6. Stir a few drops of water into the icing sugar to make a thick icing, then drizzle it over the top. Leave to set before serving.

Preparation time: **30 minutes**

Cooking time: **12 minutes**

Calories per portion: **218**

Pumpkin and coconut verrines

750 g / 1 lb 10 ½ oz / 6 cups culinary
  pumpkin or butternut squash, peeled
  deseeded and cubed

2 tbsp maple syrup

1 tsp ground mixed spice

400 ml / 14 fl. oz / 2 cup canned coconut
  milk, chilled unopened

2 tsp stevia

1 tsp coconut or vanilla extract

250 ml / 9 fl. oz / 1 cup 0% fat Greek yogurt

1 tbsp sugar-free cake sprinkles

1. Steam the pumpkin for 12 minutes or until
   tender to the point of a knife.

2. Transfer it to a food processor and add the
   syrup and mixed spice, then blitz to a smooth
   puree. Leave to cool, then chill in the fridge.

3. Open the can of coconut milk upside down
   and pour off the thin watery layer (this can
   be used in a different recipe). Scoop the thick
   creamy layer into a bowl and add the stevia
   and coconut or vanilla extract.

4. Whip with an electric whisk until it reaches
   the consistency of whipped cream. Beat the
   yogurt to loosen it, then fold it into the
   coconut cream.

5. Transfer the coconut mixture to a piping bag
   fitted with a large star nozzle. Pipe a third of
   it into six dessert glasses and top with half of
   the pumpkin puree.

6. Pipe half of the remaining coconut mixture
   on top, followed by the rest of the pumpkin.
   Pipe a final swirl of coconut on top of each
   dessert, then garnish with sprinkles.

7. Serve immediately.

MAKES: 6

Preparation time: **1 hour**

Cooking time: **45 minutes**

Calories per portion: **467**

Wholemeal apple pecan tarts

125 g / 4 ½ oz / ½ cup low-fat
  margarine, cubed

250 g / 9 oz / 1 ²/₃ cups wholemeal plain
  (all-purpose) flour

75 ml / 2 ½ fl. oz / ⅓ cup maple syrup

2 large egg whites, lightly beaten

1 ½ tbsp sunflower oil

1 tsp vanilla extract

½ tsp ground cinnamon

125 g / 4 ½ oz / 1 cup pecan nuts,
  coarsely ground

2 tbsp dark rye flour

3 small eating apples, halved

1. Preheat the oven to 200°C (180°C fan) / 400F /
    gas 6.

2. Rub the margarine into the flour and add
    just enough cold water to bind. Chill for
    30 minutes then roll out and use to line four
    individual tart cases. Prick the pastry with a
    fork, line with clingfilm and fill with baking
    beans or rice.

3. Bake for 10 minutes then remove the clingfilm
    and baking beans and cook for another
    5 minutes to crisp.

4. Reduce the oven temperature to 180°C
    (160°C fan) / 350F / gas 4.

5. Whisk the maple syrup with the egg whites,
    oil, vanilla extract and cinnamon in a bowl,
    then stir in the pecan nuts and rye flour.

6. Divide it between the pastry cases and top
    each one with half an apple. Bake the tarts
    for 30 minutes.

7. Serve warm or at room temperature.

Preparation time: **15 minutes**

Chilling time: **4 hours**

Calories per portion: **213**

Chia and mango puddings

50 ml / 1 ¾ fl. oz / ¼ cup maple syrup

600 ml / 1 pint / 2 ½ cups soya milk

100 g / 3 ½ oz / ½ cup chia seeds

2 ripe mangoes, peeled, stoned and chopped

125 g / 4 ½ oz / ¾ cup pomegranate seeds

50 g / 1 ¾ oz / ½ cup jumbo porridge oats

1. Dissolve the maple syrup in the soya milk, then stir in the chia seeds. Cover and chill in the fridge for 3 hours, stirring every 30 minutes.

2. Divide the chia mixture between six glass jars and lean them at a 45° angle in the fridge. Chill for at least 1 hour or overnight.

3. Put the mango in a liquidizer and blend until smooth. Stand the chia jars upright and spoon in the mango puree.

4. Top the jars with pomegranate seeds and oats and serve immediately.

SERVES: 4

Preparation time: **20 minutes**

Cooking time: **30 minutes**

Chilling time: **2 hours**

Calories per portion: **176**

Crème brûlée

400 ml / 14 fl. oz / 1 ²/₃ cups skimmed milk

1 vanilla pod, split lengthways

4 large egg yolks

2 tbsp stevia

1 tsp cornflour (cornstarch)

2 tbsp granulated sugar

1. Preheat the oven to 140°C (120°C fan) / 275F / gas 1.

2. Put the milk and vanilla pod in a saucepan and bring slowly to simmering point, stirring occasionally.

3. Whisk the egg yolks, stevia and cornflour together until smooth, then gradually incorporate the hot milk, whisking all the time. Discard the vanilla pod.

4. Put four individual gratin dishes or ramekins in a roasting tin and pour enough boiling water around them to come halfway up the sides.

5. Pour the custard into the gratin dishes, then transfer the tin to the oven and bake for 20 minutes or until the custards are set around the outside with just a slight wobble in the centre. Leave to cool to room temperature, then chill in the fridge for at least 2 hours.

6. When you're ready to serve, sprinkle a teaspoon of granulated sugar over the surface of each custard, shaking to get an even coverage. Caramelize the sugar with a blowtorch or under a very hot grill.

7. Serve immediately.

Preparation time: **5 minutes**
Cooking time: **30 minutes**
Calories per portion: **206**

Baked apple

1 Bramley apple

1 tbsp sultanas

1 tbsp walnuts, chopped

1 tsp low-fat margarine

½ tsp stevia sweetener

¼ tsp mixed spice

1 tbsp 0% fat Greek yogurt

1. Preheat the oven to 180°C (160°C fan) / 350F / gas 4.

2. Cut a slice off the top of the apple, then hollow out the core.

3. Mix the sultanas and walnuts with the margarine, stevia and mixed spice, then pack it into the cavity of the apple.

4. Bake in the oven for 30 minutes or until a skewer will easily slide into the centre of the apple. Serve with a dollop of Greek yogurt.

SERVES: 8

Preparation time: **1 hour 10 minutes**

Cooking time: **1 hour**

Calories per portion: **478**

Chocolate and pistachio pie

100 g / 3 ½ oz / ½ cup low-fat
  margarine, cubed

200 g / 7 oz / 1 ⅓ cups plain
  (all-purpose) flour

600 g / 1 lb 5 oz / 2 ¾ cups low-fat
  cream cheese

150 ml / 5 fl. oz / ⅔ cup reduced-fat
  soured cream

50 g / 1 ¾ oz / ¼ cup stevia

2 large eggs, plus 1 egg yolk

½ tsp almond extract

2 tbsp sugar-free white chocolate syrup

2 tbsp plain (all-purpose) flour

100 g / 3 ½ oz / ¾ cup pistachio
  nuts, chopped

50 g / 1 ¾ oz / ⅓ cup dark chocolate
  (min. 70% cocoa solids), chopped

1. Preheat the oven to 200°C (180°C fan) / 400F /
   gas 6.

2. Rub the margarine into the flour and add
   just enough cold water to bind. Chill for
   30 minutes then roll out and use to line a
   round pie dish. Prick the pastry with a fork,
   line with clingfilm and fill with baking beans
   or rice. Bake for 10 minutes then remove the
   clingfilm and baking beans and cook for
   another 8 minutes to crisp.

3. Reduce the oven temperature to 180°C (160°C
   fan) / 350F / gas 4.

4. Whisk together the cream cheese, soured
   cream, sugar, eggs and yolk, almond extract,
   chocolate syrup and flour until smooth. Fold
   in half the chopped pistachios, then spoon the
   cheesecake mixture into the pastry case and
   level the top.

5. Bake the cheesecake for 40 minutes or until
   the centre is only just set, then leave to cool
   completely in the dish.

6. Melt the chocolate in a microwave or bain-
   marie and pour it over the top. Sprinkle the
   rest of the pistachios around the edge.

SERVES : 4

Preparation time: **15 minutes**

Calories per portion: **66**

Summer berry verrines

2 tbsp icing (confectioner's) sugar

½ tsp vanilla extract

250 ml / 9 fl. oz / 1 cup 0% fat Greek yogurt

300 g / 10 ½ oz / 2 cups mixed
summer berries

4 sprigs mint

1. Whisk the Greek yogurt with the icing sugar
   and vanilla extract until smooth.

2. Divide a third of the berries between four
   glass bowls and top with a third of the yogurt
   mixture. Scatter over another third of the
   berries and spoon the rest of the yogurt
   on top.

3. Decorate the verrines with the rest of the
   berries and a sprig of mint. Chill in the fridge
   until ready to serve.

SERVES: 4

Preparation time: **15 minutes**
Freezing time: **4 hours**
Calories per portion: **67**

Cherry sorbet

400 g / 14 oz / 2 ²/₃ cups cherries, stoned,
  plus 4 whole with stalks

1 tbsp stevia sweetener

1 egg white, lightly beaten

1. Put the cherries in the freezer for 3 hours.
2. Transfer the frozen cherries to a food
   processor. Add the stevia and 50 ml of water
   and blend until smooth. Add the egg white
   and blend again, then scrape the mixture into
   a plastic tub and freeze for 1 hour.
3. Scoop the sorbet into four glasses and
   garnish each one with a whole cherry.

Treats

The idea of having a treat on a fasting day might seem like a ridiculous idea. However, when you are severely restricting your calorie intake, the odd treat can be exactly what you need to keep you on the straight and narrow and can help to satisfy any hunger pangs or cravings you may be experiencing.

All of the treats in this chapter are portable for snacking on the go.

As your diet becomes more nutritious, balanced and healthy, you should start to feel fuller for longer and have fewer cravings. Having said this, there is no reason why you should banish snacks and treats from your diet completely.

From Wholemeal Coconut Muffins and Black Forest Beetroot Brownies to a filling Oaty Date Slice or Spiced Apple Cake, you will find inspiration for delicious treats, which will stave off any pesky cravings!

S E R V E S :   1 2

Preparation time: **15 minutes**

Cooking time: **45 minutes**

Calories per slice: **313 (chocolate cake), 324
(spiced cake), 268 (strawberry cake)**

Cake trio

175 g / 6 oz. / ¾ cup unsalted butter

175 g / 6 oz / ¾ cup caster sugar

3 large eggs

175 g / 6 oz / 1 ¼ cup self-raising flour

1 tsp baking powder

FOR THE CHOCOLATE CAKE

75 g / 2 ½ oz / ¾ cup cocoa

200 g / 7 oz / 2 cups icing sugar

50 ml / 1 ¾ fl. oz / ¼ cup boiling water

FOR THE SPICED CAKE

1 tbsp mixed spice

100 g / 3 ½ oz / 1 cup icing sugar

200 g / 7 oz cream cheese

50 g / 1 ¾ oz / ½ cup walnuts, chopped

FOR THE STRAWBERRY CAKE

100 g / 3 ½ oz strawberries, sliced

50 g / 1 ¾ oz / ¼ cup caster sugar

50 g / 1 ¾ oz / ½ cup icing sugar

1. Preheat the oven to 180°C (160°C fan) / 350F / gas 4 and grease and line a 18cm (7in) round cake tin.

2. Mix together the butter and sugar until pale and gradually add the eggs to the mixture.

3. Sift the flour and baking powder into the mixture. For the chocolate cake, add 50 g of cocoa at this stage. For the spiced cake, add the tablespoon of mixed spice and stir well.

4. Pour the batter into the prepared tin and bake for 45 minutes until a skewer inserted into the centre of the cake comes out clean. Remove and allow to cool in the tin for 5 minutes then remove to a wire rack.

5. For the chocolate cake, combine the icing sugar and water in a bowl. Whisk to form a glaze and separate off ⅓ of the icing. Stir the cocoa into the remaining ⅔. Pour the chocolate glaze over the cooled cake, then decorate with the white glaze.

6. For the spiced cake, whisk the icing sugar and cheese together until light. Spread over the cooled caked and sprinkle with the chopped nuts.

7. For the strawberry, Place the sliced strawberries into a bowl with the sugar and leave to macerate for 20 minutes. Stir in the icing sugar and place on top of the cake.

MAKES : 1 2

Preparation time: **25 minutes**
Cooking time: **18 minutes**
Calories per portion: **283**

wholemeal coconut muffins

1 large egg

120 ml / 4 fl. oz / ½ cup sunflower oil

120 ml / 4 fl. oz / ½ cup skimmed milk

375 g / 12 ½ oz / 2 ½ cups wholemeal self-raising flour, sifted

1 tsp baking powder

200 g / 7 oz / ¾ cup caster (superfine) sugar

50 g / 1 ¾ oz / ½ cup desiccated coconut

1. Preheat the oven to 180°C (160°C fan) / 350F / gas 4 and line a 12-hole muffin tin with paper cases.

2. Beat the egg in a jug with the oil and milk until well mixed. Mix the flour, baking powder, sugar and all but 1 tablespoon of the coconut in a bowl, then pour in the egg mixture and stir just enough to combine.

3. Divide the mixture between the paper cases and sprinkle with the rest of the coconut.

4. Bake for 18 minutes or until a skewer inserted comes out clean.

5. Leave to cool before serving.

Preparation time: **45 minutes**

Cooking time: **40 minutes**

Calories per brownie: **320**

Black forest beetroot brownies

200 g / 7 oz / ¾ cup low-fat cream cheese

50 ml / 1 ¾ fl. oz / ¼ cup reduced-fat
   soured cream

2 large eggs, plus 1 egg yolk

½ tsp vanilla extract

2 tsp plain (all-purpose) flour

2 tbsp stevia

300 g / 10 ½ oz / 2 cups fresh
   cherries, stoned

175 g / 6 oz / 1 cup brown sugar

150 ml / 5 fl. oz / ⅔ cup sunflower oil

175 g / 6 oz / 1 ¼ cups self-raising flour

50 g / 1 ¾ oz / ½ cup unsweetened
   cocoa powder

200 g / 7 oz / 1 ⅔ cups raw beetroot, grated

200 ml / 7 fl. oz / ¾ cup beetroot juice

1 tsp arrowroot, slaked with 1 tbsp cold water

1. Preheat the oven to 190°C (170°C fan) / 375F /
   gas 5 and line a 20 cm x 30 cm (8 in x 12 in)
   cake tin with greaseproof paper.

2. Whisk together the cream cheese, soured
   cream, egg yolk, vanilla extract, plain flour
   and 1 tablespoon of stevia until smooth.
   Fold in a third of the cherries and set aside.

3. Whisk the sugar, whole eggs and oil together
   for 3 minutes until thick. Fold in the rest of
   the flour with the cocoa powder and beetroot.

4. Scrape two thirds of the mixture into the tin
   and top with the cheesecake mixture. Spoon
   the rest of the brownie mix on top. Bake for
   40 minutes or until a skewer inserted comes
   out clean. Leave to cool in the tin.

5. Put the rest of the cherries in a saucepan with
   the beetroot juice and remaining 1 tablespoon
   of stevia. Simmer for 5 minutes, then add the
   slaked arrowroot and stir until it thickens.

6. Cut the brownie into twelve squares and serve
   with the cherry sauce spooned over.

SERVES : 8

Preparation time: **25 minutes**

Cooking time: **45 minutes**

Calories per portion: **225**

Apple and blackberry cake

225 g / 8 oz / 1 ½ cups self-raising flour

1 tsp ground cinnamon

100 g / 3 ½ oz / ½ cup low-fat margarine, cubed

100 g / 3 ½ oz / ½ cup caster (superfine) sugar

1 large egg

75 ml / 2 ½ fl. oz / ⅓ cup skimmed milk

2 eating apples, peeled, cored and sliced

1 tsp icing (confectioner's) sugar

150 g / 5 ½ oz / 1 cup blackberries

1. Preheat the oven to 180°C (160°C fan) / 350F / gas 4 and line a 23 cm (9 in) round cake tin with greaseproof paper.

2. Sieve the flour and cinnamon into a mixing bowl. Rub in the margarine until it resembles fine breadcrumbs and stir in the sugar. Lightly beat the egg with the milk and stir it into the dry ingredients until just combined.

3. Scrape the mixture into the tin and press the apple slices into the top.

4. Bake for 45 minutes or until a skewer inserted comes out clean.

5. Transfer the cake to a wire rack and leave to cool completely then sprinkle with icing sugar and top with blackberries.

Preparation time: **25 minutes**

Cooking time: **35 minutes**

Calories per portion: **276**

Oaty date slice

175 g / 6 oz / ¾ cup medjool dates,
    stoned and chopped

2 ripe bananas

100 ml / 3 ½ fl. oz / ½ cup raw honey

100 g / 3 ½ oz / ½ cup low-fat
    baking margarine

450 g / 1 lb / 4 ½ cups rolled porridge oats

50 g / 1 ¾ oz / ²/₃ cup flaked
    (slivered) almonds

1. Preheat the oven to 160°C (140°C fan) / 325F / gas 3 and line a 20 cm x 30 cm (8 in x 12 in) tray bake tin with greaseproof paper.

2. Put the dates in a small saucepan with 100 ml of water. Cover and simmer for 5 minutes, then blend to a paste in a liquidizer. Scrape into a bowl and set aside.

3. Put the bananas in the blender with the honey and margarine and blend until smooth. Stir in the oats and almonds.

4. Spread half the mixture in an even layer in the tray bake tin and top with the date puree. Cover with the rest of the oat mixture, pressing down firmly.

5. Bake for 35 minutes or until golden brown. Cut into twelve squares while still warm but leave to cool completely before removing from the tin.

SERVES : 8

Preparation time: **25 minutes**

Cooking time: **45 minutes**

Calories per portion: **217**

Spiced apple cake

100 g / 3 ½ oz / ½ cup low-fat
   margarine, cubed

225 g / 8 oz / 1 ½ cups self-raising flour

100 g / 3 ½ oz / ½ cup caster
   (superfine) sugar

1 tsp ground ginger

½ tsp ground star anise

1 large egg

75 ml / 2 ½ fl. oz / ⅓ cup skimmed milk

2 red eating apples, peeled, cored and sliced

1 tsp icing (confectioner's) sugar

1. Preheat the oven to 180°C (160°C fan) / 350F /
   gas 4 and line a 23 cm (9 in) round spring-
   form cake tin with greaseproof paper.

2. Rub the margarine into the flour until it
   resembles fine breadcrumbs, then stir in the
   sugar and spices.

3. Lightly beat the egg with the milk and stir it
   into the dry ingredients until just combined.
   Scrape the mixture into the tin and press the
   apple slices into the top.

4. Bake for 45 minutes or until a skewer inserted
   comes out clean.

5. Transfer the cake to a wire rack and leave to
   cool completely.

6. Sprinkle with icing sugar just before serving.

Dear diary

It's easy to lose track of what we eat on a daily basis and, while you're trying to lose weight, it's a good idea to jot down what you've eaten and when.

This not only helps you to stick to your calorie limit on fast days but it also means you can spot days and times when keeping to the guidelines may be a little harder. Another benefit to jotting down your daily meals is that you can look back on what you've eaten when you're struggling for inspiration.

If you write things down, you simply can't 'forget' about that biscuit or that extra slice of ham you wolfed down while waiting for lunch to cook. Keeping a diary is especially important for the 5:2 diet as you'll be able to assess which days work best for you and which meals help you to get through the two fast days.

Keep a note of any exercise (both formal and informal) that you do too. This will motivate you to keep going with your new lifestyle.

Week 1

TOP TIP
Find a photograph of a celebrity whose figure you most admire and stick it on the inside of your kitchen cupboards for inspiration.

Today I weigh

Weight loss so far

Fast days

Fast Day 1	
Breakfast	
Lunch	
Dinner	
Snacks	
Exercise	
Total Cals	

Fast Day 2	
Breakfast	
Lunch	
Dinner	
Snacks	
Exercise	
Total Cals	

Exercise log

How I feel

week 2

Today I weigh

Weight loss so far

Fast days

Fast Day 1	Fast Day 2
Breakfast	Breakfast
Lunch	Lunch
Dinner	Dinner
Snacks	Snacks
Exercise	Exercise
Total Cals	Total Cals

TOP TIP

Find a routine booster that works for you.
It could mean deep conditioning your hair once
a week, or setting time aside for that facemask.
Choose something that takes only a few minutes
but makes you feel good about yourself for
hours afterwards.

Exercise log

How I feel

Week 3

Today I weigh

Weight loss so far

Fast days

Fast Day 1	
Breakfast	
Lunch	
Dinner	
Snacks	
Exercise	
Total Cals	

Fast Day 2	
Breakfast	
Lunch	
Dinner	
Snacks	
Exercise	
Total Cals	

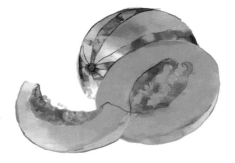

TOP TIP

Take your mind off food and get historical.
You walk past that museum or art gallery every
day – now's the time to step inside. You will see
and learn so much fascinating stuff, you will
forget about food for a while!

Exercise log

How I feel

TOP TIP
Dig it! If you have a patch of land, give it the once over. Clearing a patch of soil can be quite a liberating experience. Even more exciting, you can think about what you're going to plant in the area. Flowers? Vegetables? This could be the start of grow-your-own!

week 4

Today I weigh

Weight loss so far

Fast days

Fast Day 1	
Breakfast	
Lunch	
Dinner	
Snacks	
Exercise	
Total Cals	

Fast Day 2	
Breakfast	
Lunch	
Dinner	
Snacks	
Exercise	
Total Cals	

Exercise log

How I feel

week 5

TOP TIP

Find a weight loss buddy who's trying to shed a few pounds too. That way you can encourage each other and swap recipes. Even if none of your local friends are slimming, there are bound to be some Facebook or Twitter mates that can help motivate you.

Today I weigh

Weight loss so far

Fast days

Fast Day 1	
Breakfast	
Lunch	
Dinner	
Snacks	
Exercise	
Total Cals	

Fast Day 2	
Breakfast	
Lunch	
Dinner	
Snacks	
Exercise	
Total Cals	

Exercise log

How I feel

Today I weigh

Weight loss so far

Fast days

Week 6

Fast Day 1	
Breakfast	
Lunch	
Dinner	
Snacks	
Exercise	
Total Cals	

Fast Day 2	
Breakfast	
Lunch	
Dinner	
Snacks	
Exercise	
Total Cals	

TOP TIP

Liven up your cold drinks by freezing low calorie squash and adding them to water. Use two or three flavours and mix and match. Imagine how tasty orange and blackcurrant-flavoured ice cubes make that glass of water.

Exercise log

How I feel

week 7

Today I weigh

Weight loss so far

Fast days

Fast Day 1	
Breakfast	
Lunch	
Dinner	
Snacks	
Exercise	
Total Cals	

Fast Day 2	
Breakfast	
Lunch	
Dinner	
Snacks	
Exercise	
Total Cals	

TOP TIP

Try a new exercise on top of all your daily activity. Look out for news of new classes on local notice boards. How about zumba or line dancing? Many of them are pay as you go so there's no need to sign up for a whole year.

Exercise log

How I feel

TOP TIP

Go to work on an egg. Incorporate an egg-based meal into one of your fast days this week. Eggs are wonderful little things – they're cheap, packed with protein and keep you feeling nice and full.

Week 8

Today I weigh

Weight loss so far

Fast days

Fast Day 1	
Breakfast	
Lunch	
Dinner	
Snacks	
Exercise	
Total Cals	

Fast Day 2	
Breakfast	
Lunch	
Dinner	
Snacks	
Exercise	
Total Cals	

Exercise log

How I feel

week 9

TOP TIP
Get merry with berries. Soft fruits such as blackberries, strawberries and raspberries are all jam-packed with vitamin C and fibre and are very low in calories. If you have a sweet craving, pop open a box of frozen raspberries and eat them like sweets.

Today I weigh

Weight loss so far

Fast days

Fast Day 1	
Breakfast	
Lunch	
Dinner	
Snacks	
Exercise	
Total Cals	

Fast Day 2	
Breakfast	
Lunch	
Dinner	
Snacks	
Exercise	
Total Cals	

Exercise log

How I feel

week 10

Today I weigh

Weight loss so far

Fast days

Fast Day 1	
Breakfast	
Lunch	
Dinner	
Snacks	
Exercise	
Total Cals	

Fast Day 2	
Breakfast	
Lunch	
Dinner	
Snacks	
Exercise	
Total Cals	

TOP TIP
Spend some time preparing for your fasting day.
Think ahead about what you would like to eat
within your calorie limits and look forward to it!

Exercise log

How I feel

week 11

Today I weigh

Weight loss so far

Fast days

Fast Day 1	
Breakfast	
Lunch	
Dinner	
Snacks	
Exercise	
Total Cals	

Fast Day 2	
Breakfast	
Lunch	
Dinner	
Snacks	
Exercise	
Total Cals	

Exercise log

How I feel

Week 12

Today I weigh

Weight loss so far

Fast days

Fast Day 1	
Breakfast	
Lunch	
Dinner	
Snacks	
Exercise	
Total Cals	

Fast Day 2	
Breakfast	
Lunch	
Dinner	
Snacks	
Exercise	
Total Cals	

Exercise log

How I feel

staying slim

Getting slim is one thing; now you want to be sure you can stay at your wonderful new weight. Many dieters put the pounds back on because they revert to old eating habits and they start to get lazy about keeping active.

You don't want to undo all that hard work, do you? Make sure the 'new' you becomes the 'always' you with these tips:

• Rather than abandoning the whole 5:2 principle all together, why not go 6:1 and have six days of ordinary eating a week, allowing one day per week to fast? Now that you are used to fitting fasting days into your routine, you'll find this an easy way to maintain your new weight. Use your one fast day a week to revisit all the recipes that helped you through in the first place.

• Keep up the activity levels, rain or shine. No matter what the weather is like, keep up the brisk walks. They're great for toning, for boosting your mood and for putting a smile on your face.

- Don't forget why you did the 5:2 diet in the first place. You don't want to backtrack now, do you?

- If you've gone down a clothes size (or two), have a great big wardrobe clear out. Package up any clothes that are too large and either sell them at a car boot sale, on an auction site or be generous and donate them to charity. Think how good that makes you feel!

- Incorporate some of the 5:2 recipes into every day menus. They make a good balance on days when you've had a hefty lunch or you're late getting up.

- Take the compliments. When people tell you how good you're looking, hold your head up and thank them. It's all too easy to dismiss it when someone says something nice to us. But go right ahead and smile. You worked hard. You deserve the praise.

- Set an example. If you have children or young people in your life, let them see you enjoying fruits and vegetables, swooning over salads and crooning over red cabbage. They will soon see how happy and healthy eating a varied, colourful diet makes you feel.

- Keep track. Weigh yourself once and week and pat yourself on the back every time you maintain weight.

Before

After